IDEAS & HOW-TO

Stone
Landscaping

Meredith® Books
Des Moines, Iowa

Better Homes and Gardens® Ideas and How-To: Stone Landscaping
Editor: Michael McKinley
Associate Design Director: Todd Emerson Hanson
Contributing Graphic Designer: Matthew Eberhart,
  Evil Eye Design, Inc.
ContributingWriter: Kate Carter Frederick
Contributing Project Editor: Megan McConnell Hughes
Copy Chief: Terri Fredrickson
Copy Editor: Kevin Cox
Publishing Operations Manager: Karen Schirm
Senior Editor, Asset and Information Management: Phillip Morgan
Edit and Design Production Coordinator: Mary Lee Gavin
Art and Editorial Sourcing Coordinator: Jackie Swartz
Editorial Assistants: Kaye Chabot, Renee McAtee
Book Production Managers: Pam Kvitne, Marjorie J. Schenkelberg,
  Mark Weaver
Contributing Copy Editor: Nancy Humes
Contributing Proofreaders: Pegi Bevins, Sara Henderson, Lida Stinchfield
Contributing Cover Photographer: Ed Gohlich
Contributing Illustrator: Robert LaPointe
Contributing Indexer: Donald Glassman
Contributing Researcher: Susan Ferguson

Meredith® Books
Editor in Chief: Gregory H. Kayko
Executive Director, Design: Matt Strelecki
Managing Editor: Amy Tincher-Durik
Executive Editor: Benjamin W. Allen
Senior Editor/Group Manager: Vicki Leigh Ingham
Senior Associate Design Director: Ken Carlson
Marketing Product Manager: Brent Wiersma

Executive Director, Marketing and New Business: Kevin Kacere
Director, Marketing and Publicity: Amy Nichols
Executive Director, Sales: Ken Zagor
Director, Operations: George A. Susral
Director, Production: Douglas M. Johnston
Business Director: Jim Leonard

Senior Vice President: Karla Jeffries
Vice President and General Manager: Douglas J. Guendel

Better Homes and Gardens® Magazine
Editor in Chief: Gayle Goodson Butler

Meredith Publishing Group
President: Jack Griffin
Excutive Vice President: Doug Olson

Meredith Corporation
Chairman of the Board: William T. Kerr
President and Chief Executive Officer: Stephen M. Lacy

In Memoriam: E.T. Meredith III (1933–2003)

IDEAS & HOW-TO
Stone Landscaping

All of us at Meredith® Books are dedicated to providing you with information and ideas to enhance your home and garden. We welcome your comments and suggestions. Write to us at: Meredith Books, Garden Editorial Department, 1716 Locust St., Des Moines, IA 50309-3023.

Note to the Readers: Due to differing conditions, tools, and individual skills, Meredith Corporation assumes no responsibility for any damages, injuries suffered, or losses incurred as a result of following the information published in this book. Before beginning any project, review the instructions carefully, and if any doubts or questions remain, consult local experts or authorities. Because codes and regulations vary greatly, you always should check with authorities to ensure that your project complies with all applicable local codes and regulations. Always read and observe all of the safety precautions provided by manufacturers of any tools, equipment, or supplies, and follow all accepted safety procedures.

Contents

The Joy of Stone

Of all the materials available for landscaping, stone has the most natural-looking, and enduring qualities. With its inherent versatility, structural integrity, and powerful impact, stone inspires endless design possibilities. Stone adds value and beauty to your home's setting whether you integrate it into a functional part of the landscape or use it as a strictly ornamental outdoor element.

In this book you will find a comprehensive array of ways to use stone in the landscape, from the ground (paths, patios, edging) up (steps, walls, accents). Look to the photographs for insights about stone building techniques and how they affect the finished look. For instance, note how stones are set in the ground, spaced, fitted together, mortared, and stacked.

Whether stone is sawn, chiseled, tumbled, or polished, it demonstrates how skill and artistry can merge with the medium to create personal, artful additions to the landscape. The creative process begins here as you consider the options, from a vast world of stone types to a wide range of building projects that will enhance your home and landscape.

Used in building and landscape construction for thousands of years, stones tell silent stories that grace and enrich lives when they are included in the landscape. These igneous, sedimentary, and metamorphic characters bring various colors, textures, lines, and degrees of strength to their hardworking and aesthetic tasks. But the type of geologic formation matters less than the way you plan to use the stone. This book will enable you to recognize the differences between sandstone and granite, rubble and cut stone, flagstone and steppers, cobbles and pavers, pebbles and pea gravel. Whether combined with plants, water, wood, or other building materials, stone always looks at home in the landscape.

Large stone slabs form a sturdy walkway to the front door of this seaside home. Functioning both as a path and gentle steps, the blue-gray slabs are a perfect complement to the blue ocean beyond.

The style of these simple, stacked stone steps pairs nicely with the informal hillside plantings surrounding them. The pleasing curve of the steps leads the eye into the garden beyond.

A combination of gravel and boulders forms a well-drained planting space perfect for drought-tolerant plants.

Simple flagstone steppers draw visitors off the patio and into the garden. Stone is an excellent choice for long-lasting paths in the landscape.

When you choose stone indigenous to your region, it will fit the setting naturally and be one of the most economical options. Rely on local stone suppliers and landscape architects, designers, or comparable professionals to guide you in the process of selecting appropriate stone materials for your projects. A treasure trove of stone is available in all regions, but the selection of stone types and their names vary from place to place. In addition to natural stone, you'll find an expanding selection of stonelike materials made from concrete, composites, and other materials.

Each chapter that follows is packed with ideas and inspiration to help you identify potential features for your landscape and plan their creation. You will soon discover how every stone pathway, patio, wall, or other project will be uniquely yours as you select a type of stone, a building technique, and a design suited to your home site.

While the aesthetic characteristics of stone contribute largely to the finished look of a project, its design and building technique come to bear as well. Throughout this book, you'll find tips to guide you in selecting the best materials along with design advice and construction notes to help ensure your project's success.

The planning and design information in each chapter will help you prepare for construction, whether you intend to handle the stone landscaping project yourself or enlist a contractor. You'll learn the basics of working with stone and discover the timeless pleasure that comes with it, whether the project entails your physical or creative energy—or both!

Cut stone and flagstone come together to give this striking path a formal feel. Artfully stacked flagstones create the massive fountain.

1 Paths

A path or walkway establishes and defines a journey. Whether distinguished as an entry, exit, or transition, a well-planned and beautifully constructed path leads the way. As a route from one point to another, a pathway links home and landscape—or areas within a landscape—functionally as well as aesthetically.

When you choose stone for a pathway, you will enhance the setting with stone's natural character and enduring charm. Stone suits most architectural styles with options ranging from gravel to cobblestone, flagstone, cut stone, and more. Each material, along with different methods of path construction, can be matched to specific needs of the household and landscape to create a lasting garden element.

Walk This Way

Every path should have a purpose. When planning and designing a pathway for your landscape, begin by thinking about how you will use it and then imagine how you want it to look. Before you determine whether the path should be straight or curved, what materials to use, or how to construct it, consider the types of stone available for pathmaking and how each would fit into your landscape.

On these pages you'll find a multitude of possibilities for pathways to help you with the process. As you peruse the options from rustic fieldstone to elegant cut stone, think about how you could use them—singly or in combination. Some questions that will help you design the most practical pathway include: Where will it begin and end? Is it necessary to add small paths off the main path to direct traffic? How will it work to the advantage of the natural terrain—whether relatively flat or gently sloping—and will it drain well? Do existing plantings and soil present special problems with logistics or drainage that the path can help solve? How will the path help beautify the landscape and lead you to lovely views within it? This is just the beginning.

A casual flagstone walkway winds past petite pocket gardens en route to a large perennial planting beyond. A curvaceous pathway like this one paired with annuals and perennials creates an element of surprise by masking the destination until a traveler draws near.

The pea gravel covering this pathway creates a pleasing crunch with every footstep. Each type of gravel has a unique sound underfoot; consider the sound of the gravel when selecting a material.

Simple stepping-stone paths add to the established look and feel of a garden and are also practical. The majority of weeding and plant care chores can be accomplished from a pathway, which reduces soil compaction.

Stepping-stones take on a formal appearance when uniformly shaped stones are arranged in a pattern. This striking stepping-stone path to a garage was created with light gray paving stones. The geometric design complements the lines of the garage door.

Stepping-Stone Paths

For simplicity of design, ease of installation, and affordability, lay your path in a single line of stepping-stones. Few paths appear as natural and inviting, whether leading across a lawn or garden or circling a pond. Set in gravel, bark mulch, turf, or other plantings, stepping-stones give the landscape a relaxed, informal character.

As a secondary type of path that you may not take every day, one made with stepping-stones often seems the ideal way to link parts of the landscape. For example, visitors are led step-by-step to a secluded garden room or around one side of the house where the way isn't obvious. A few steps link the kitchen garden and the house in the most direct route possible to help minimize the dirt tracked indoors. Well-placed steppers make space for weeding amid a billowing perennial garden.

Where lawn or other parts of the landscape become worn to the soil by foot traffic, there's potential for stepping-stones. The way may be short—a stone or two at a landing or where foot traffic begins or ends—or long around a water garden or to an outbuilding.

Simple steppers placed in a seemingly random way will lead the eye along the pathway and entice you to follow it. The type and spacing of the stones encourage you to slow down and look around as you stroll through the garden, across the yard, or into a more natural landscape such as a wooded area.

Stepping-stones form both the patio and path in this landscape. Enticing visitors into the garden, a ribbon of blue-gray stepping-stones extends from the patio into a shaded perennial bed. For continuity in the garden, consider using the same material for all hardscape features.

An uneven pathway like this narrow stepping stone walkway encourages strolling and is best as an auxiliary path instead of a main thoroughfare through the landscape.

Designing a Stepping-Stone Path

A path formed with stepping-stones should match natural walking stride to ensure comfortable footing. Large stones with generous gaps may force awkward giant steps; small stones may force tiptoeing or even cause stumbling.

Steppers measuring at least 14 to 16 inches across will accommodate most walkers comfortably. Manufactured or cut stones with a uniform size and shape lend themselves to even placement. Aim to place irregular flagstones as horizontally as possible, with their longer dimensions extending across the path for best results.

Most often, steppers are placed in a single file and accommodate individual strollers. Staggering the stones broadens the path. Create an inviting path entry by placing two or three stones side by side, then narrowing to single steppers along the course. Finish the path with a group of two or three stones placed side by side. Alternatively start and stop the path or signal a change in direction using stones about 1½ times larger than average. Creating wider areas by doubling or tripling the stone is a good way to make a circular path. It also works well when you want to create a wayside, such as a bench, water feature, or other place to stop beside a path.

The purple and maroon chrysanthemums along this stepping-stone path are sure to stop visitors in their tracks. Don't be afraid to nestle plants right next to a path. Guests are more likely to stop and admire pathside blossoms than those that grow several paces away from the walkway.

Garden art draws the eye and the feet. Design paths to safely deliver wandering feet to garden attractions. The stepping-stone walkway skirting this armillary sphere allows visitors to appreciate it up close.

Moss and irregularly shaped stepping-stones combine to create an informal path leading toward a patio. Use small stepping-stones in single file for a narrow path or place them side by side for a wider walkway.

LAY A STEPPING-STONE PATH

Flagstone steppers are often placed in single file (right). To broaden the path and create an informal look, choose steppers with an oblong shape and stagger them (left).

Low-growing creeping thyme, a fragrant herb, forms a dense green mat, choking out any weeds that attempt to grow between these stepping-stones. Blanketing the soil of the path-to-be with heavy-duty landscape fabric before setting the stepping-stones is another effective method of keeping weeds at bay.

Placing Stepping-Stones in the Landscape

Plan to set stepping-stones on or in the ground, depending on the surroundings. In the lawn it's easy and wise to set steppers level with the ground so you can mow over and around them.

If you plan to lay a stepping-stone path in a soft bed of gravel or bark mulch, prevent weeds (and continual irritation) by covering the path-to-be with heavy-duty landscape fabric. The extra time spent laying the landscape fabric will save hours of weeding later. Once you have positioned the stepping-stones, cut around each one to make openings in the fabric. Then excavate at least 2 inches and make a sand base for each stone. After the stones are set, spread a contrasting bed of gravel or bark around them to make the steps clearly visible.

Keep in mind that if you want to move a wheelbarrow or other outdoor equipment over a soft-dirt path, you might want to space the steppers closer together or use especially large stepping-stones for satisfactory results.

Stepping-stones also give you a way to walk across a garden without trampling on the plants and compacting the soil. Set in a planting area, steppers should be a bit above ground level to promote drainage.

Regularly shaped and placed steppers form a predictable walking surface. Eyes are free to wander into the color-rich beds along the path without the concern of missing a step.

Selecting Stepping-Stones

Almost any stone with a relatively flat surface is a good candidate for a stepping-stone path. Flagstone, cut stone, and manufactured stonelike steppers make equally effective paths. Select large, flat, similar-size stones. Cut stone and manufactured steppers offer these characteristics with consistency. Fieldstones can be used as steppers as long as they're large enough and have a flat side.

For stability and longevity, steppers should be 1½ to 2 inches thick. You'll want stones with enough texture to provide ample traction. If you handpick the stones, avoid ones that are concave; they will collect rain and soil and might become slippery when wet. Stones with recesses will hold water and may split in cold climates where freezing and thawing occur.

Natural flagstones bring a sense of timeless beauty to the landscape. Flagstones work extraordinarily well for gracefully curving paths or steps cut into a gentle slope to make it more easily traversable. Soft, porous sandstone and shale can be used as short-term steppers. They will deteriorate over time; plan to replace them as needed to maintain a safe path. Cut stone steppers and large pavers are more suitable for formal and geometric designs.

Exploration beckons as these sandstone steppers extend from a spacious patio. Several hues of sandstone steppers are available to complement a landscape. When setting stepping-stones, situate them as horizontally as possible to prevent stumbles.

Large stepping-stones are handy in densely planted gardens where plants have a tendency to spill onto the walk. The large stones help maintain a narrow, yet serviceable, path.

The large stepping-stone in the foreground denotes a fork in the path. Visitors can further explore the garden by traveling left or right on the narrow steppers laid directly into the garden soil. The stones can be rearranged on a whim but one disadvantage is that the stones will settle over time.

Installing Stepping-Stones

Installing stepping-stones is simple. First, determine the location and general outline of the path by laying out two parallel lengths of garden hose as a guide. Lay the stones on the ground, adjusting their placement to create pleasing curves, if desired, and suitable spacing. Walk on them using your usual stride to check their placement. Your feet should land near the centers of the stones.

Then cut the sod or score the soil around each stepper with a heavy-bladed knife or small spade. Move the stone aside and dig out the area to the depth of the stone. Most stepping stone paths do not require a gravel base unless bedded in persistently moist soil or in an area subject to extreme frost. In these cases excavate an additional 2 to 4 inches, lay a 1- to 2-inch base of gravel, and top it with a 1- to 2-inch layer of sand. Place each stone, settling it and adding sand if necessary to level it. Otherwise adding a 2-inch base of sand under each stone will aid drainage and minimize settling. Most steppers settle over time. Pry them out and reset them in additional sand as needed.

If stones are set too low or they settle too much over time, they may harbor moisture, soil, or gravel, creating a hazard. Correct the problem by tipping up each stone and adding and leveling enough sand to raise the stepper.

A dense carpet of creeping thyme rambles around these limestone steppers. A fast-growing perennial, thyme quickly creeps between stones, forming a fragrant groundcover.

INSTALL STEPPING STONES

Sand is a valuable addition to a stepping-stone pathway. It aids drainage, minimizes settling, and is helpful as you work to level the steppers during installation. Spread a 1- to 2-inch layer of sand in the base of the excavated stepping-stone location. Smooth the sand and place the stepper. Add or remove sand to create a level surface.

Create a graceful, curving path like this one with the help of two garden hoses. Use the hoses to outline the borders of the path, adjusting them until you find a curve that pleases your eye. Set the stepping-stones between the hoses.

Perhaps gathered from the field beyond, the
fieldstones that make up this path appear perfectly
at home. The color, shape, and texture of fieldstone
vary by region. Visit a local stoneyard to learn
about stones that are native to your area.

Fieldstone and Cobblestone Paths

The most rustic-looking pathway materials come from fields and streams across the country. Formed naturally and tumbled by time and glaciers, fieldstones reflect the geology of the region where they are found. Whether smooth and rounded or rough and broken-edged, fieldstones may be spherical, egg-shape, oblong, or flat on both sides. The flat fieldstone proves ideal for the most casual and natural-looking paths around, while rounded fieldstones make outstanding edging.

Fieldstones set into the ground form a quaint pathway that immediately appears timeworn. For this reason, a fieldstone path suits country homes as well as cottage gardens. But the stones' uneven surfaces present potential hazards, especially at night, and benefit from lighting. The uneven crevices between the stones provide hospitable places for groundcovers to grow.

Cobblestones also bring the appeal of a durable, age-old material to the landscape. The small, handsplit square pavers are as reliable for high-traffic walkways as they continue to be for old-world streets. Recycled old cobblestones and newly manufactured ones come in various sizes and colors that inspire patterned designs. Their flat surfaces form an even, level pathway. As a classic pathmaking material, cobblestones are equally adaptable for their charm in an urban landscape or their luxury as part of a new home.

A combination of flat- and round-surface stones works together to pave the area around a tranquil water feature. The rustic charm of the fieldstones softens the formality of the area.

Petite fieldstones, all carefully laid to form a meticulously even surface, draw visitors into this lush garden. A layer of sand beneath the stones allows them to be raised or lowered with ease to form a level surface.

Selecting Fieldstones and Cobblestones

Comparably durable fieldstones and cobblestones bring a sense of strength and permanence to the landscape. Historically both materials were collected from the surroundings and arranged into roads and walkways. The cobblestones now salvaged may have served as paving surfaces for hundreds of years.

Cobblestones give a pathway instant character, whether their antique patina has come after centuries of use or from the tumbling process of modern manufacturing. New or old, most cobblestones are square or rectangular. Typically granite, salvaged stones have a dark patina and worn appearance. Although they're becoming harder to find, most antique cobblestones are 4- to 6-inch cubes; some resemble large bricks.

You'll find new cobblestones in a variety of sizes and colors, including gray, black, yellow, and pink. Cobblestones made from materials such as sandstone, limestone, and granite offer the same consistent appearance as other prized landscape pavers.

Fieldstones, on the other hand, display the multicolor hues of their origins. You can also purchase sorted fieldstones of a particular type, such as bluestone. The range of fieldstone sizes and shapes is endless. One other quality sets fieldstones apart: They often come with the moss, lichen, and soil that shared their place in nature.

New rectangular and square cobblestones lend this path the same old-world character as their hard-to-find antique counterparts. Visit a local stone yard to view a selection of the many different types of new cobblestones available for purchase.

Combine different color fieldstones to achieve this unique look. White stones, most likely limestone, are juxtaposed with mottled bluestone.

CONSIDER THE SURFACE

Minimize the hazard of slipping on a path. Coarse-textured stone works best in areas that tend to stay wet. To help water drain instead of puddle, a flagstone or cut stone walk should be sloped to one side; a gravel or cobblestone path should be crowned in the center. If you live in a region where snow is common, consider this when selecting material for a path. The unevenness of a fieldstone path is less than accommodating for snow shoveling. Selecting fieldstones with a flat side for the surface of your pathway makes it more user-friendly—especially where snow falls. Large, flat stones will be easiest to clear.

Small, round fieldstones are perfect for plantings of low-growing flowers. The white blossoms of sweet alyssum decorate this fieldstone path. This self-seeding fragrant plant stands up to foot traffic.

Winding through perennials and shrubs, this fieldstone path appears to rise naturally from the soil. The uneven surface of the path makes it unsafe at dusk and at night but is perfectly fine for careful travel during daylight hours.

Installing Fieldstones and Cobblestones

A pathway of fieldstones or cobblestones, dry-laid on a bed of sand, offers amazing longevity. Fieldstones present an economical option for pathmaking, while cobblestones sit at the higher end of the price spectrum. If you have your eye on attractive stones in a field or creek nearby, be sure to get permission from the landowner before harvesting any material.

A natural-looking path should begin with excavation to allow the stones' surface to sit just above ground level. The stones will settle with time. A base of landscape fabric, topped with a 2-inch layer of gravel followed by a 2-inch layer of sand, will hasten drainage and help deter weeds.

For high-traffic areas, set the stones more closely together and pack sand, granite dust, or a dry-set compound (3 parts sand to 1 part cement) between them to help minimize places where heels may get caught. Some professionals prefer to set cobblestones in mortar for a durable pathway.

Fitting fieldstones' natural contours together in a beautiful, functional pathway is part of their charm. A fieldstone path that includes all sizes of stones looks most natural. It works best to place the largest stones as you would steppers—to accommodate your natural stride—and fit a range of smaller stones between them.

One reason people choose cobblestones for a walkway is because they can be laid in patterns, including basket-weave, herringbone, and fan-shape designs. Cobblestones also make handsome edging for a variety of paths, from gravel to cut stone. If cobblestones don't fit your walkway budget, you might appreciate their appearance as edging instead.

CREATE A DECORATIVE LOOK

Laying cobblestones or fieldstones in a deliberate pattern, based on the materials size, shape, or color, creates a more decorative effect. A tightly set, uniform edge alone adds a more finished touch.

1. Edging stones Cobblestone cubes outline the edge of the path. A 4-inch layer of gravel topped with a 2-inch layer of sand lifts the cubes 2 inches above the adjoining path.

2. Path stones The path is paved with cobblestone cubes. The base of the path is a 2-inch layer of gravel topped with a 2-inch layer of sand. Several stones were cut with a stone saw to maintain the grid pattern.

Formal plantings pair nicely with uniformly shaped cobblestones. These square cobbles are complemented by trimmed boxwood hedges. A rustic twig pergola adds informal charm.

Planting Along a Path

Plants provide natural partners for pathways. They visually soften hard edges and break up sprawling expanses of paving. The living colors in the form of blooms and foliage brighten and enliven a walkway. What's more, fragrant plants such as creeping varieties of thyme and mint add another pleasurable dimension.

You'll find a wealth of planting possibilities to create desired effects, from soft carpet to lush edge. Some plants thrive in the usually dry tight spots between stepping-stones or flagstones. Others benefit from more space and moisture, typically prevalent along a gravel path. The lowest growers form a dense cushion or tickle the toes as they withstand footsteps. Other plants aim higher, filling in as edging. Most great plants for pathside planting spread slowly to fill in gaps between stones.

Select plants suited to the prevailing conditions of your yard, including soil, sun, and moisture. It helps to know a bit about a plant's growing habits, so if you haven't grown a particular plant before, ask about it at the nursery or do a little research. Does it grow slowly and need some TLC at first? Will it tolerate drought and survive if rain is scarce during its first year in your yard?

Moss, while lush looking, is widely regarded as a garden thug. As such, it can grow too well and become invasive—spreading into garden beds and lawn.

GROW STEPPABLE PLANTS ALONG PATHS

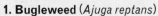
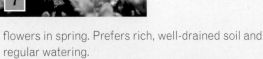

1. Bugleweed (*Ajuga reptans*)
Moderate traffic, sun to part shade, Zones 4–9. Matting, quick spreader, 3 inches tall with blue to purple flowers in spring. Grows best in sandy loam. Mow after flowering.

2. Creeping thyme (*Thymus serpyllum*)
Moderate traffic, sun to part sun, Zones 4–9. Matting, moderate-spreading fragrant herb, 2 inches tall, with white, pink, or purple flowers in summer. Prefers well-drained soil and occasional watering.

3. Dwarf periwinkle (*Vinca minor*)
Heavy traffic, part shade, Zones 5–7. Moderate spreader, 5 inches tall with lavender or white blooms in summer. Prefers rich, moist soil.

4. Pearlwort (*Sagina subulata*)
Heavy traffic, sun to part shade, Zones 4–10. Mounding, mosslike foliage, ½-inch tall with tiny star-shape white flowers in spring. Prefers rich, well-drained soil and regular watering.

5. Miniature stonecrop (*Sedum spectabile*)
Heavy traffic, sun, Zones 4–8. Matting, slow-growing succulent, 2 to 3 inches tall, mostly with yellow or red blooms, various foliage colors depending on variety. Evergreen or nearly evergreen. Drought tolerant.

6. Spotted dead nettle (*Lamium maculatum*)
Moderate traffic, shade to part shade, Zones 4–8. Green-and-white mottled leaves form a dense mat, 3 to 8 inches tall with white or pink flowers in summer. Prefers well-drained soil.

7. Woolly thyme (*T. pseudolanuginosus*)
Moderate to heavy traffic, sun to part sun, Zones 6–9. Matting, moderate spreader, ½-inch tall, flowers minimally, if at all. Prefers well-drained soil.

Silvery-gray woolly thyme and vibrant green creeping thyme grow together to create a lush, fragrant weed barrier around flagstone steppers. Thyme grows best in well-drained soil and tolerates dry conditions. It will grow to form a dense carpet in full sun.

A roving flagstone walkway pairs perfectly with an overflowing urn planted in the middle of the path. Give a path an always-been-there look by spacing the stones 2 or 3 inches apart and planting low-growing perennials in the crevices.

Lawn turf forms fuzzy green halos around these flagstones. Achieve a similar look by sprinkling quality grass seed on the soil between stones. Lightly rake the soil to ensure the seed and soil make contact. Water gently until the seeds send up shoots. Groom by mowing.

Flagstone Paths

As a traditional favorite for stone pathways, flagstone looks handsome in all kinds of settings. It suits almost any style of architecture, especially when the landscape's design reflects the native environment of the region. The reddish sandstone popular for paving in the Southwest, for example, echoes the surrounding desert and mountains.

The flat slabs or flags—especially when large—pave sizable expanses of landscape with natural elegance. Flagstone is an excellent choice for primary and secondary pathways. It can stand up to heavy foot traffic as well as hard use from wheeled garden equipment.

Flagstone is a popular choice for patios and makes equally attractive coordinating pathways. While flagstone alone creates an aesthetically rich path, it also combines well with other materials, such as gravel and beach stones. Gaps of ⅜-inch or wider between flagstones support plantings, such as Irish moss and sandwort, which tolerate close quarters.

Count on a flagstone walkway to be sturdy, whether set and filled with sand or mortar. Set tightly or mortared, flagstone can enhance a more formal setting. When spaced generously, set with sand, or used as stepping-stones, flagstone demonstrates its versatility and creates a more casual effect.

Sandstone flags reflect the tones of the surrounding dry lands and mountains in this Southwest garden. The yellow-brown stones are an appropriate foil for the colorful perennials and shrubs. Gravel mulch between and around the stones keeps weeds at bay.

Designing a Flagstone Path

Flagstone's flat face makes it ideal for paving. Although small flags conform somewhat better than large ones to minor variations in terrain, flagstone works best on sites that are mostly flat or gently sloping.

The irregular shapes of flagstone proves suitable in free form and geometric designs. To increase the formality of a design, keep straight edges to the outside of the path or use geometric edging such as brick. When fitted tightly and shaped with a clean edge, the flagstone path also has a more formal appearance. Widely spaced stones create a more casual effect.

The size of the flagstones as well as the way the path is made will affect the finished appearance. Large flagstones cover a surface more quickly than smaller ones, but they are also more costly, heavy, and difficult to set. Smaller gardens call for smaller stones or a mix of large and small. When using a mix of sizes, consider scattering the placement of large stones, as you would for a stepping-stone path.

Flagstone paths, like stepping-stone walkways, provide planting opportunities. Low-growing perennials will quickly blanket the soil between flags, creating a soft surface that contrasts nicely with the stones.

Stone edging, commonly called "bullet edgers," gracefully finish the perimeter of this path. Brick, cast stone, or any uniformly shaped stone can be used to form a tidy edge along a flagstone path.

CREATE ATTRACTIVE CURVES

Curving paths are more natural and pleasing to the eye. Curves may be necessary to accommodate trees, planting areas, structures, and even slopes. They can also heighten a sense of mystery and reward walkers with changing vistas. A path doesn't have to curve to be effective. To plot the most graceful curves for a path, outline the edges using garden hoses. Then mark the edges with flour or powdered chalk.

Large and small flagstones unite in this meandering path. Small flags are especially useful in the construction of curving paths. They readily fill the gaps between large stones to make a gradual curve.

A flagstone path extends like an artful rug at the base of a twig bench. A pathside perch can be as simple as a generous log or a plush bench—choose a style that suits you and your garden.

Selecting Flagstone

You'll find an array of flagstone that differs in appearance and durability. Most flagstone is split from sedimentary rock, such as bluestone and slate, which is formed in layers and lends itself to fracturing. The stones are available in thicknesses from 1 to 2 inches or more. Thicker stones (more than 1½ inches) hold up best under heavier use. Thinner flagstones work fine if laid on a concrete base and set with mortar.

Other common types of flagstones include limestone, quartzite, sandstone, and granite—each with its own qualities. Widely available sandstone, in hues of tans and reds, offers a grainy, nonslip surface and wears over time with use. Extremely durable granite—especially flat and smooth—comes in many colors from white to black.

Flagstones of a lighter hue, such as limestone, make a pathway more visible in a shady area. The darker tones of slate and some granite can have a cooling effect when contrasted with plantings in warmer, sunnier areas. In hot climates, dark-color stone may become uncomfortable for bare feet. Any stone that contains quartz or mica will sparkle in sunshine—an extraordinary quality in any landscape. If your landscape design already uses variations in shape and texture, you might choose to minimize additional contrasts in color.

SIX GREAT FLAGSTONE CHOICES FOR YOUR NEXT PATH

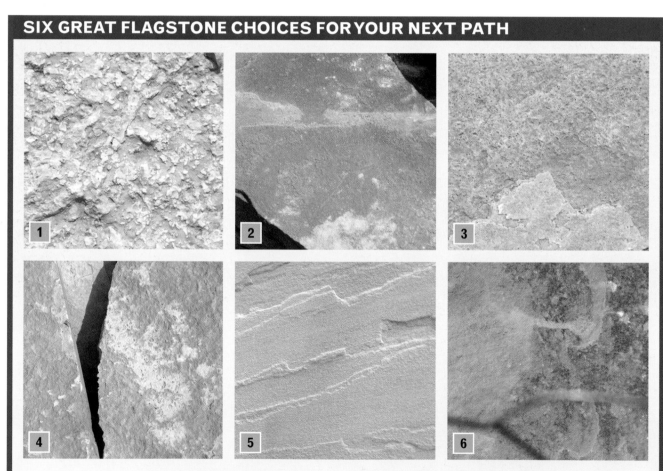

Finding a variety of flagstone options is not difficult. Visit local stoneyards or building centers and consider possibilities that will complement your landscape in terms of color and texture. When possible, choose a stone that is native to your region; it is most likely to withstand challenging weather conditions with ease.

1. Bay de Noc Gray bands of color run through this light brown limestone. Native to Michigan.

2. Colorado red This red-orange sandstone is long-lasting and withstands freeze-thaw cycles. Native to Colorado.

3. Fond du Lac Available in many shades of white, gray, and tan, this limestone is commonly found in Wisconsin.

4. Iowa buff The rich cream color of this limestone is notably consistent. It often has a very flat surface, making it a good choice for paths and patios. Native to Iowa.

5. New York blue Popular for its wide range of colors, New York blue is a hard sandstone available in shades of blue, gray, brown, and copper. Native to the East Coast.

6. Tumbled bucksin Native to the Southwest, this sandstone has a weathered appearance.

Frequently used service paths like this extending alongside a house are great candidates for flagstone. A sand base will limit settling, keeping the stones level for years.

Mortar unites these sandstone flags. Although more time-consuming to install than a dry-laid path, a mortared path resists settling and maintain a level surface for decades.

Bluestone flags play off the blue-green shutters beyond. Consider dominant landscape colors when choosing flagstone and help a path blend into the surroundings by choosing a color of stone that complements prominent landscape features.

Installing Flagstones

The finished look of a flagstone pathway will always show off the irregular shapes of the stones. But it will vary depending on how the stones are laid—dry-set in sand or wet-set with mortar. Do-it-yourselfers can install either without much difficulty. The process of fitting the irregular stones together compares with completing a jigsaw puzzle, whichever method is followed.

For a dry-set pathway, flagstones are laid on a 6-inch base of gravel followed by a 2-inch layer of sand. Once the stones are settled on the sand, more sand is packed in between the stones. Dry-set surfaces heave and return without consequences from changes in ground temperature—a plus in cold winter climates. Just as groundcovers such as creeping phlox and sedum will grow readily among the stones, so will weeds until the desirable plants fill in. Allow grass to grow between flagstones only if you're willing to mow or trim it regularly.

Solid mortared surfaces need a concrete base to prevent them from cracking. The concrete requires a 6-inch base of gravel. A mortared path requires minimal lawn care—only occasionally sweeping or blowing.

It is best to install large pathside features, such as this gate and fence, before laying the path so you don't disturb a path's sand base. When it is necessary to excavate in a pathway, firmly tamp the dislodged soil back in place to form a solid base and top with sand before relaying the stones.

CUT FLAGSTONE

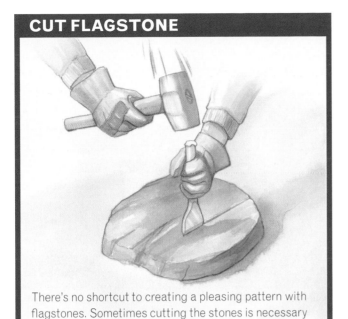

There's no shortcut to creating a pleasing pattern with flagstones. Sometimes cutting the stones is necessary to fit them better or to shape contours. Here's how to cut flagstone:

First mark the cut with pencil or chalk. Then score the stone using a stone chisel and hammer or a circular saw with a diamond blade. Finally break off the waste portion using a mason's hammer and small sledge.

Install a narrow, 10- to 15-foot-long path like this one in a weekend. Excavating the soil to create a firm base for the gravel and sand layers is the most labor-intensive portion of the project.

Fit together like a puzzle, a straight-edge flagstone path like this requires patience to construct. A few of the stones were likely cut using a chisel and hammer or a circular saw to achieve the nearly straight edge. The trimmings were then pieced into the path.

Gravel Paths

A gravel or loose-stone path fits into any landscape, from a modest Midwestern farmstead to a stately manor-style home. A wide, straight, primary gravel pathway to the main entrance of the home creates a sophisticated look. On the other hand, a narrow, meandering gravel path flows casually through a landscape. Gravel creates an unequaled sense of flow and expansiveness.

Gravel offers a variety of advantages, beginning with an array of textures and colors. Loose stone conforms to minor variations in terrain—crushed material holds well on gentle slopes. Most gravel drains well and dries out quickly, making it popular for garden paths and ideal for areas with tree roots. Economical and easy to install, gravel requires only occasional weeding and limited replacement. It is suited to all climates.

A loose-stone path also adds another element to the landscape not provided by other surfaces: the crunching sound of it underfoot. Most gravel is not kind to bare feet and presents a navigational challenge for anything on wheels.

Gravel travels. The shifting aggregate in a loose-stone path migrates from designated walkways unless it is confined with edging. Even when edged, the durability of a gravel path varies with traffic and the size of the aggregate. Over time, if enough stones are kicked away and carried off in shoes or packed into the ground, bare spots may give way to weeds. Yet it is possible to make a hard, compacted path of crushed gravel that's as permeable as soil and is inhospitable to weeds.

Loose stone is quick and easy to install and is the best choice for many serpentine paths. Simply establish an eye-pleasing curve using two garden hoses or thick rope, excavate as necessary, and spread the gravel. The earthtone gravel used for this path blends into the landscape, allowing nearby plants to shine.

Ending at a simple stone bench, this loose-stone path illuminates the shaded retreat. Highlight dense shade with light-color loose stone. Beware of bright white stone; it can easily appear too stark. Gray or cream-color stone is an excellent, natural-looking choice.

The informal nature of loose stone contrasts admirably with the formality of brick in this walled garden. The simplicity of the path directs attention to the flower-filled borders.

Designing Gravel Paths

If you're looking for versatility in your landscape, gravel is a great choice. Loose-stone pathways complement and contrast with the use of aggregate in a range of types and textures. An imaginative design takes advantage of the colors and sizes of gravel available, combining them in a pattern or another creative way.

Just think of the possibilities: Crumbles of dark-gray decomposed granite form hard, straight paths between structures in a formal setting. Rosy-quartz chunks create a pleasant contrast of pastel ribbon laid next to evergreens. A winding path of multihued river rock edged with similarly weather-rounded but larger fieldstone inspires a relaxed response. Crushed white limestone highlights the way to walk through a shaded area, and the path even glows in moonlight.

Regardless of the size and type of gravel you use, consider edging the path if you want to prevent the loose stones from drifting away. For the ultimate natural look, use stone—cut or tumbled—partially buried, as an edge. Other edging options include concrete pavers, brick, metal, or flexible resin. Pressure-treated landscape timbers, though often used, will crack and deteriorate.

Tidying a gravel path is as simple as lightly running a rake across the surface to collect leaves, twigs, and other landscape debris. After removing debris, run the rake over the path again to level the loose stones and retrieve any pebbles that tumbled into adjacent beds.

When gravel paths end at a dwelling, the gravel often accompanies visitors across the threshold. Minimize the mess by wrapping the entryway with a cut stone or flagstone pad. Much of the gravel will dislodge from shoes on the pad.

WRAP AN ENTRYWAY WITH A STONE PAD

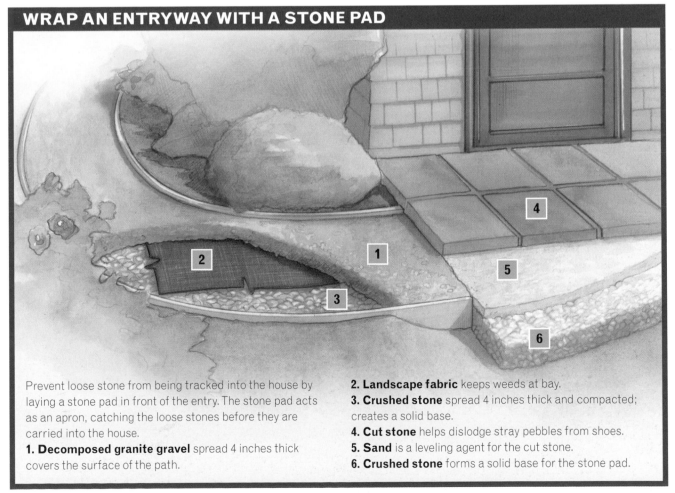

Prevent loose stone from being tracked into the house by laying a stone pad in front of the entry. The stone pad acts as an apron, catching the loose stones before they are carried into the house.

1. Decomposed granite gravel spread 4 inches thick covers the surface of the path.

2. Landscape fabric keeps weeds at bay.

3. Crushed stone spread 4 inches thick and compacted; creates a solid base.

4. Cut stone helps dislodge stray pebbles from shoes.

5. Sand is a leveling agent for the cut stone.

6. Crushed stone forms a solid base for the stone pad.

Selecting Gravel for a Path

Once the pathway is designed, select the type, texture, size, and color of gravel for it. Choose from two types of gravel: crushed or natural. The mechanically crushed stuff (mostly granite, quartz, and limestone) has angular edges that shift against one another underfoot and lodge in place, making it one of the best choices for a path. Available in a variety of sizes, the most common for pathways is ⅜- or ¾-inch gravel, but you could choose up to 1½ inches. If too large for a path, the gravel will shift more underfoot than you would like.

Natural gravel—smooth and rounded—is collected from natural deposits, then sorted by size from fine pea gravel to coarser river rock and larger beach stones. The tumbled edges of natural gravel slip and roll. As smaller aggregate settles into the subbase, the surface stones tend to migrate more with use. For walking comfort, choose ¼- to ¾-inch gravel.

You'll find gravel in single colors from white to black and the hues in between. Some aggregate contains a mixture of different colors that complement one another. Choose colors carefully. Bluestone may look enticing in the sample box at the stoneyard but too vivid when installed. White rock may contrast too starkly with adjoining flowerbeds, especially in a sunny location. If you have a hard time deciding which gravel will best suit your landscape, bring samples home and try them in place.

Natural gravel can vary greatly in color. If you request a delivery of natural gravel from a local stone yard, be sure before it is unloaded that the stone color is what you had in mind.

SEVEN GREAT GRAVEL CHOICES FOR YOUR NEXT PATH

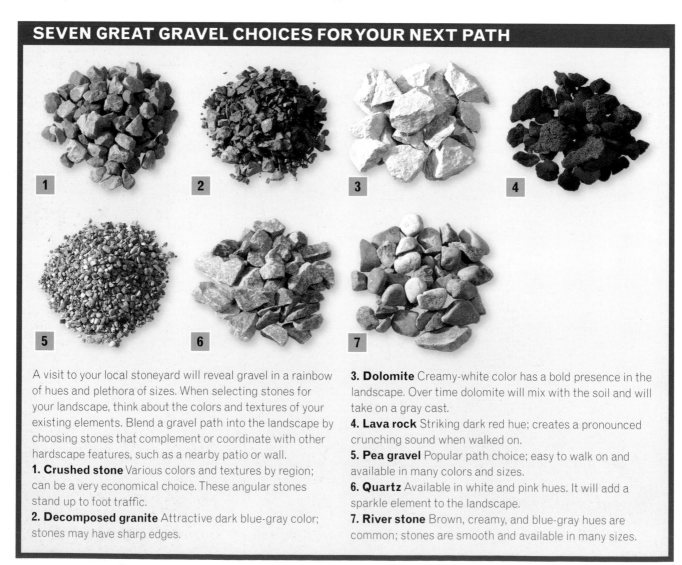

A visit to your local stoneyard will reveal gravel in a rainbow of hues and plethora of sizes. When selecting stones for your landscape, think about the colors and textures of your existing elements. Blend a gravel path into the landscape by choosing stones that complement or coordinate with other hardscape features, such as a nearby patio or wall.

1. Crushed stone Various colors and textures by region; can be a very economical choice. These angular stones stand up to foot traffic.

2. Decomposed granite Attractive dark blue-gray color; stones may have sharp edges.

3. Dolomite Creamy-white color has a bold presence in the landscape. Over time dolomite will mix with the soil and will take on a gray cast.

4. Lava rock Striking dark red hue; creates a pronounced crunching sound when walked on.

5. Pea gravel Popular path choice; easy to walk on and available in many colors and sizes.

6. Quartz Available in white and pink hues. It will add a sparkle element to the landscape.

7. River stone Brown, creamy, and blue-gray hues are common; stones are smooth and available in many sizes.

(Right) Pea gravel is available in a host of earthtones unique to the region where it was quarried. Light-brown gravel decorates this Georgia garden. Visit your local stone yard to see what colors of pea gravel are available in your area.

(Below right) Heavy-duty landscape fabric nestled beneath the decomposed granite of this roving path prevents weeds and seedlings from the nearby perennial beds from taking root in the middle of, the walkway.

(Below left) Stabilize loose gravel on an incline with the help of barriers laid horizontally across the path every few feet. Functioning like a dam on a river, the barriers prevent much of the gravel from collecting at the bottom of the incline.

A thin strip of metal edging prevents gravel from spilling into the beds adjoining the linear portions of this path. Flexible resin edging borders the curved segment of the walkway.

BUILD A GRAVEL PATH

A simple combination of crushed stone, landscape fabric, gravel, and edging combine to create a lasting gravel path. Multipurpose landscape edging available at home centers borders this path. Large stones, bricks, or pavers also make suitable edging for a gravel path.

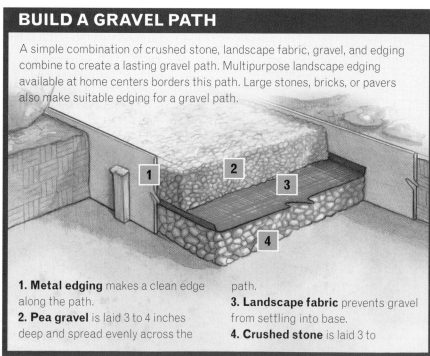

1. **Metal edging** makes a clean edge along the path.
2. **Pea gravel** is laid 3 to 4 inches deep and spread evenly across the path.
3. **Landscape fabric** prevents gravel from settling into base.
4. **Crushed stone** is laid 3 to

Installing Gravel Paths

A few tricks ensure a well-made gravel path that will provide a stable, quick to drain, and lasting place to walk.

To begin, the pathway should be excavated 6 to 8 inches. Laying a 4-inch base of road-grade gravel provides excellent drainage and a firm foundation. Topping that with landscape fabric prevents soil and gravel dust from seeping into the base and making it less able to drain. The fabric also deters weeds.

The edging you choose will help hold the landscape fabric in place. If you prefer not to use hard edging—if the gravel borders a perennial bed, for instance—remember that gravel will be displaced and must be replenished. In this case, hold the fabric in place with landscape spikes and top with gravel.

You can also top the landscape fabric with a 1-inch subbase of fine-washed sand or select gravel for the pathway that includes fine particles and gravel dust. Either method helps prevent sharp gravel from punching holes in the fabric, and both materials compact, reducing the downward migration of the surface gravel.

To keep your gravel path looking its best, rake or blow it in spring and fall to remove leaves and other debris. Pull any weeds. Then rake the gravel to level it.

Lush pathside plantings like these will litter the path from time to time. Simply rake away debris with a flexible leaf rake. Snow, on the other hand, is tough to clear from a gravel path. Keep the gravel in place by skimming off the majority of the snow, leaving a ½-inch layer on the path surface.

Cut Stone Paths

Cut stone provides an orderly, flat, stable, and user-friendly surface. It comes from the same natural rock as flagstone, but it differs in shape and aesthetics. Flagstones are irregular. Cut stones are more uniform, with straight-sawn edges, square corners, and flat sides. The stone—including tumbled marble, tumbled granite, travertine (extremely hard limestone), quartzite, and limestone—is quarried and cut to various sizes, from large slabs to brick-size pavers.

Cut stone lends itself to a variety of situations, from an elegant and straightforward main entryway to a more random and rough-hewn curving walkway. Cut stone pathways with straight edges and flat surfaces seem more like sidewalks and are particularly well suited to modern-style homes or stately older ones. Pavers are often chosen for extremely durable, weather-resistant walks such as a main access to the garage and pool decks because they are easy on bare feet.

The finished look of a cut stone path depends on the type of stone, its size and texture, and the way the stones fit together. Usually the tighter the joints, the more elegant the look, the less hazard of tripping, and the lower the maintenance. Cut stone works best in flat, level areas. Laying cut stone where there are even subtle grade changes is more labor intensive and costly.

The installation method that you choose will affect the finished look of the walkway. Neatly cut stone works well for the same method of installation as flagstone—in sand or dry mortar over gravel and sand, or in wet mortar over concrete. The size consistency of cut pavers makes them relatively easy to install. Dry-set in sand, cut stone and cut stone pavers demonstrate a high degree of resilience and durability in extreme conditions, compared to concrete, asphalt, and brick.

A random-laid bluestone path cuts through a perennial garden in an inviting way. Creeping thyme has begun to fill in between the stones.

Limestone slabs set in an even pattern and seamed with grass link the landscape with the linear front entry of the house. A veneer of limestone tile covers the steps and front porch, continuing the theme.

Cast-stone pavers mimic the look of cut stone. Combine these budget-friendly pavers into intricate designs, like the diamond pattern climbing the vine-clad front walk of this home.

An Asian-style garden called for a traditional stone path, but the budget necessitated the use of stonelike concrete pavers. The path's design enhances its stony intention.

The straight edges of these massive cut stonelike pavers are a pleasing contrast to the curve of the grand oval door frame and gently curving stucco wall. The pavers' hue complements the stucco. Many different colors of cut stone are available.

Designing a Cut Stone Path

The regularity of cut stone's geometric shapes adds a dignified, orderly flow to garden paths. In general, larger, uniform stones with straight or angular edges set in a precise pattern suggest formality. Smaller, irregularly set stones have a more casual look. Combining stones of different sizes or colors and leaving an irregular edge creates a relaxed effect.

Begin planning a cut stone walkway by shopping first, then focusing on design. Familiarize yourself with the various types of available cut stone. Sandstone, for instance, wears down under heavy use, while porous marble absorbs moisture and crack in climates that have freeze-thaw cycles. Smooth slate or marble become slick when wet and could be risky for a walkway.

Knowing the available sizes of the cut stone you plan to use will help you determine the pathway's width and length. Combine sizes of stones if you like, mixing three sizes for best results. Even if you use only one size of square stones, you will have design options—even rows, staggered rows, or diagonals. Additional sizes and shapes multiply your design possibilities.

Joints are another important part of the overall look and function of a cut stone path. Uniform, aligned joints enhance the orderly effect and are easier to achieve than when working with flagstone.

If curves and turns are desired, cut stones prove adaptable—especially for diagonal designs and angular turns. More cutting—and expense—is required for a curving walk.

Choose an irregular edge or edge your path with another size or type of cut stone. Edging isn't essential unless small pieces could break off.

CHOOSE A PATTERN FOR YOUR PATH

Enhance the beauty and style of your pathway by determining the pattern of the cut stone. Design your path's pattern on paper before it is installed onsite.

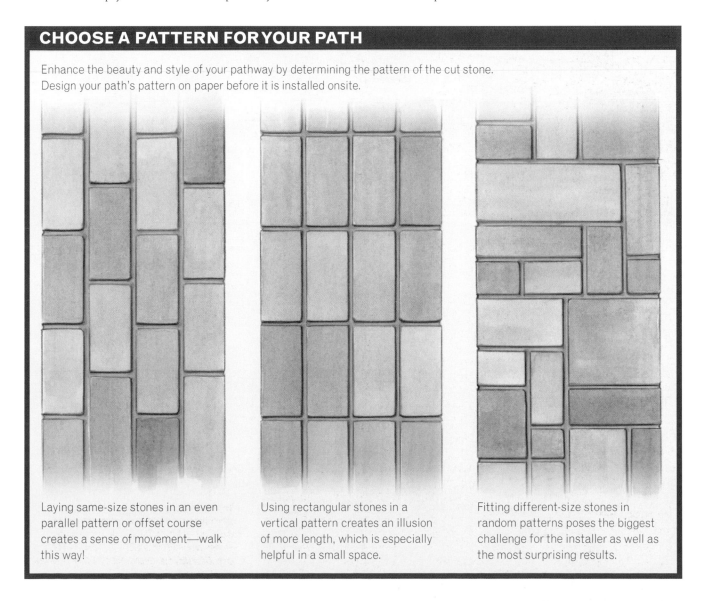

Laying same-size stones in an even parallel pattern or offset course creates a sense of movement—walk this way!

Using rectangular stones in a vertical pattern creates an illusion of more length, which is especially helpful in a small space.

Fitting different-size stones in random patterns poses the biggest challenge for the installer as well as the most surprising results.

Selecting Cut Stone for a Path

Cut stone is quarried and cut on the top, bottom, and sides by large stone saws. Pieces often come in standard lengths, ranging from approximately 1 foot to 4 feet, and different thicknesses. Choose 2-inch-thick stone for a walkway that must withstand heavy traffic without cracking or breaking. Keep in mind that the thicker and heavier the stones, the harder, slower, and costlier the installation. And the more uniform the stones' thicknesses, the more likely an even, level path will result.

Though cut stone is one of the costlier options for landscaping, cut native limestone will be less expensive than cut bluestone, for example. Keep an eye out for stonelook pavers made from concrete or a combination of concrete and recycled materials.

Consider the stone's color. For example, choose from gray-blue (bluestone) to various hues of white, tan, and red (limestone, quartzite, granite, and sandstone) to deep, sometimes slightly iridescent, black (slate).

You'll also find a range of surface textures. Some have a rough finish that aids traction. The texture may have been created by exposure to a torch or a pneumatic tool. Others have been distressed by a tumbling process or given a matte finish by sandblasting. A honed surface, if glossy or reflective, would be too slippery for a path.

Designed to resemble cut stone, these pavers are manufactured from a combination of stone and other materials. Cut stone pavers come in a wide array of colors, sizes, shapes, and textures.

A jigsaw pattern of cut stone forms an elegant entryway and adjoining walk for a traditional-style home. The straight, flat surface makes for easy maintenance year-round.

LIGHT THE WAY

Lighting highlights a pathway, making you and your visitors feel more sure-footed and welcome after sunset. Low-voltage and solar-powered lighting is easy to install yourself and creates a diffused light. At home centers you'll find an array of lighting fixtures to complement any style of landscape and house. Whatever type of path lighting you choose, install it before the walkway is constructed, if it requires wires.

Cut stone paths have a strong visual presence. Cut stones' geometric shapes give a formal look to pathways, while their straight edges

BUILD A DRY-SET CUT STONE PATH

If drainage is a problem in the area of your cut stone path, excavate to a depth of 10 to 14 inches and lay a 4- to 6-inch bed of crushed stone. Top the crushed stone with the materials listed below.

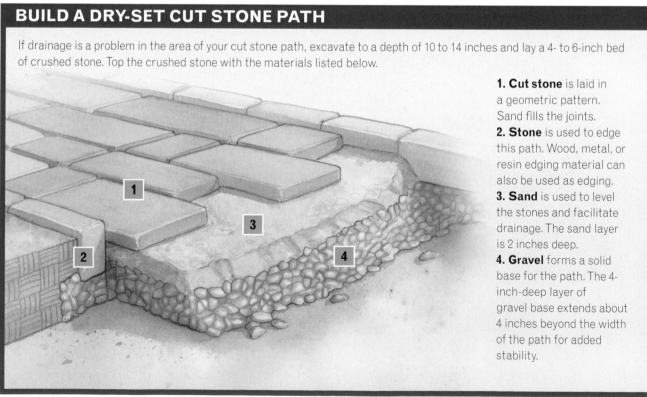

1. Cut stone is laid in a geometric pattern. Sand fills the joints.

2. Stone is used to edge this path. Wood, metal, or resin edging material can also be used as edging.

3. Sand is used to level the stones and facilitate drainage. The sand layer is 2 inches deep.

4. Gravel forms a solid base for the path. The 4-inch-deep layer of gravel base extends about 4 inches beyond the width of the path for added stability.

Installing a Cut Stone Path

Dry-set, cut stone installations call for moderate skill, while mortared paths prove more difficult. Mortar is too thick for narrow (1/16- to 1/2-inch) joints, but the stone can be mortared to a concrete slab and the joints filled with fine sand. Cut stone less than 1½ inches thick holds up best when laid on concrete.

Dry-set paths laid in sand may need weeding, resanding, and resetting over time. Consider planting low-growing creeping varieties of thyme, mint, or sedum in the cracks or aim for tight-fitting stones to minimize maintenance. Wet-set or mortared walks on concrete may wear away or pit with exposure to weather extremes and may shrink or crack over time.

Careful site and base preparation is essential for lasting construction. When excavated 8 to 12 inches deep, the soil surface should grade slightly away from the house and the center of the path. Deeper excavation is necessary in cold and wet climates to minimize shifting and settling of the area. The gravel base for a path, whether dry or wet-set, should extend 4 to 8 inches beyond the edge of the path to provide stable support for the stone as well as any edging.

To minimize the formality of a design, allow irregular edges. Otherwise, edge your path with additional cut stone, loose stone, or decorative tile, depending on the look you desire. Most cut stone paths are massive enough that they may not require edging to hold them in place. If your path runs along a garden bed, set edging to form a low border for the planting area and keep soil and mulch from spreading onto the walkway.

Hand-cut stone pieces salvaged from old buildings and roadways form the path to this bench. These found objects add historic or artful character to a landscape.

Mixed Material and Mosaic Paths

There are no rules in landscape design that say you can't combine materials in a pathway. After all, inside your home you likely have more than one type of flooring—carpet in the living room, tile in the kitchen. Different choices of flooring are appropriate when the use of the space is different, whether indoors or outdoors.

A combination of materials creates interest and helps ease transitions between different spaces. When you're adding a new path to an established place, a mix of materials allows you to blend the new with existing types of paving. The result will fit in and have a long-established appearance.

Combining two or more materials, such as cut stone with gravel or flagstone with brick and concrete, accomplishes the job with style. A mosaic, made from stones laid in patterns, exudes artistry. Mixed materials and mosaics allow you to express your personality and create an ambience in your home's surroundings.

Paths that contain a range of colors and textures draw attention, so they may be the best option for moving from one part of the landscape to another or providing a decorative landing at an entryway. Mixing materials can help you fit a pathway into an oddly shaped area, while a mosaic of various pebbles and small stones welcomes as well as any finely woven rug.

The best attributes of stepping-stones and gravel unite. The flagstone stepping-stones give the pathway a meandering, informal look and the gravel defines the edges of the walkway. A thin strip of edging runs along each side of the path to confine the gravel.

Pebble mosaics celebrate the unique nature of stone. Pebbles in a multitude of shapes, sizes, and colors are meticulously arranged to create this walkable work of art.

Gravel increases the width of this stepping-stone path. The swath of gravel will prevent nearby plants from encroaching on the path, making it too narrow for foot traffic. A layer of landscape fabric keeps weeds at bay.

Designing a Mixed Material or Mosaic Path

Add appeal to any landscape by mixing different kinds of stone with other materials or composing pebble-mosaic paths. No matter the size of the project, random shapes and varied contours that come with a mix of materials bring handwrought character to a setting.

Use these aspects to your advantage, depending on the statement you wish to make. A path that combines boldly contrasting materials or incorporates rich color encourages visitors to stop and experience the drama. More subtle combinations have a way of moving walkers along, perhaps without noticing what's underfoot because the design works so well to complement and unify the surroundings.

Mixed material and mosaic pathways take many forms. Setting flagstone pieces widely apart and filling the gaps with a single color of river stone causes the shapes of both materials to stand out. Adding brightly colored recycled-glass gravel to a design takes it to a higher level of aesthetics. A mosaic, by its intricate nature, proves compelling whether as ornamental details that crop up in the wide gaps of a flagstone path or as a one-of-a-kind accent.

A mixed material or mosaic path may have a casual or rustic appearance, but it follows a definite design. These types of pathways may take more planning and time to create, but the results will reflect your effort.

Slices of tree trunk form the steppers in this rustic river rock path. The wood steppers will deteriorate over time, but they are simple and economical to replace.

PATH WIDTHS

A primary or main pathway leading to and from the house should be wide enough—4 feet is best—to allow two people to walk easily side by side.

Secondary pathways that lead out into the landscape, either branching off from main paths or existing on their own, can be narrower: 18 inches accommodates a lone walker.

Spanning nearly 4 feet, this wide flagstone and gravel path will easily accommodate two people walking side-by-side.

Designing Mixed Materials and Mosaics (continued)

Personalized touches give any home landscape its individuality. Paths created with mosaics or mixed materials give you a prime opportunity to express yourself with stones gathered on hikes and travels. This is your chance to work your favorite blue-gray beach pebbles into the landscape where you'll enjoy them most. When someone prefers cut stone pavers and someone else wants concrete, both can be satisfied with this approach.

Be wary of overmixing single materials. When in doubt, choose a simple design over a busy one. Grouping materials or repeating them in a pattern gives a design continuity. In turn, the walk will inspire a greater sense of restful pleasure if it does not feature a hodgepodge of materials in a chaotic display. Play opposite textures or colors off each other, if you like, but do it at regular intervals.

Keep in mind that color, while artful, draws attention. A bit of color, mixed into a pattern of neutrals or repeated here and there, will be more effective than color overdone. Contrast between colors and textures also strengthens and highlights a design. Use contrasts to create interesting highlights and patterns.

The bottom line: Combining materials saves money. It may enable you to use a variety of stone leftovers from other landscaping projects.

Flagstone steppers branch off this flagstone path. Steppers and gravel have an informal feel and are a great choice for secondary walkways.

A naturally rocky landscape easily converts to a mixed material path. Lichen-covered outcroppings line the edges of this gravel and cut stone walk.

Enjoy the art of a mosaic path, without dedicating days to construction, by weaving together small mosaics and flagstones. Build a base as you would for a pebble mosaic; lay the flagstones and then fill the gaps with pebble mosaics.

BUILD A PEBBLE MOSAIC

A beautiful mosaic stops you in your tracks. The intricacy of the design is a foil for the ease of construction. Mosaics, like all stone projects, consist of carefully prepared base layers.

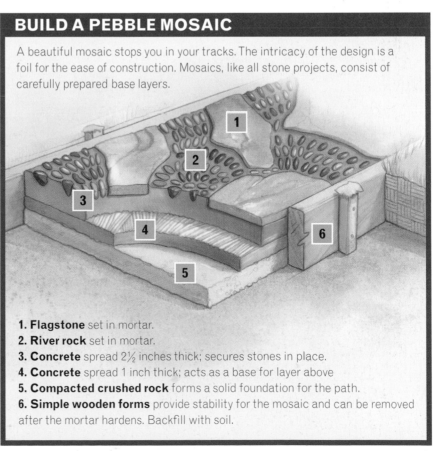

1. **Flagstone** set in mortar.
2. **River rock** set in mortar.
3. **Concrete** spread 2½ inches thick; secures stones in place.
4. **Concrete** spread 1 inch thick; acts as a base for layer above
5. **Compacted crushed rock** forms a solid foundation for the path.
6. **Simple wooden forms** provide stability for the mosaic and can be removed after the mortar hardens. Backfill with soil.

Bright blue tile, river rock, and rectangular pavers form a striking medallion in the middle of a sea of gravel. Add character to paths by incorporating unique elements, such as this blue tile, into the design.

SETTING A PEBBLE MOSAIC

Mortar, made from a premix or blended from 1 part portland cement and 3 parts sand, glues a pebble mosaic together. Pack wet mortar between the stones, then gently rinse with a garden hose sprayer to wash away the excess. Cover the concrete with a plastic sheet and keep it moist while it cures slowly and completely for a month.

Flagstones and cobblestonelike pavers are arranged side by side to create this curbside welcome mat. A small project like this is a fun way to combine different paving materials from your landscape.

Installing Mixed Material and Mosaic Paths

For pathways of mixed materials, prepare the base as you would for flagstone (a 6-inch gravel base topped with 2 inches of sand).

For mosaics, prepare a bed of crushed rock (4 to 6 inches deep) plus a layer of concrete (1 to 2 inches deep). Flexible edging makes a satisfactory frame for a mosaic and helps hold it in place. Mortar sets the stones securely.

When planning a mosaic, take time to sketch it on paper. Beautiful designs may incorporate several colors of similar-size pebbles or a broader palette, plus larger beach stones, tiles, or other material.

Tightly packed and evenly set, a pebble mosaic forms a smooth surface. Well-finished, minimally visible mortar makes the mosaic sturdy and most pleasing.

A simple pattern of gray and black river rocks set in mortar form this therapeutic walkway that has a massaging feel on the soles of your feet.

Landscape Visit: A Soothing Walk

Just as a well-designed pathway adds beauty and function to a landscape, an especially thoughtful design has a way of invigorating body, mind, and spirit. In this case, when the groundwork was laid for a labyrinth—a continuously winding path—tailored to fit a South Carolina landscape, it transformed an open terrace into a secluded garden-encircled lawn. But that was only the beginning.

Designed to encourage walking meditation, the labyrinth enables people to relax and contemplate as they move through the landscape. It enhances enjoyment of the surroundings as walkers take in the stillness and reconnect with nature. Typically a solitary walker moves along the path in quiet reflection, but children often race around the bends, laughing out loud. From quiet reflection or raucous joy, the path accommodates every mood.

A labyrinth takes people on a journey of turns, winding around the landscape to a center and back. This classic circuit labyrinth, a 3,500-year-old design, has seven circuits from perimeter to center.

(Right) The formally designed path invites night strolling, when moonlight reflects off the pale edging stones.

(Below right) The labyrinth design is complemented with seating areas and a profusion of perennials and shrubs that bring seasonal color to this setting.

(Below left) A stone cross divides four turns in the labyrinth. The final turn leads to the center of the design.

Landscape Visit (continued)

Examples of labyrinths around the world date back thousands of years. Unlike traditional mazes, with branching paths and confusing dead ends, labyrinths focus the walker's attention on the path and one's steps. Adaptable to home landscapes, patterned labyrinths have become widely popular as part of therapeutic site design. Incorporated into a holistic design, the deliberate path might amble among plantings, up and down inclines, and past impressive scenes. Invariably a path made for walking meditation helps complete the landscape or a sanctuary.

This Carolina Low Country labyrinth, laid with sod and edged with white river rock, invites individual strollers. The pathway's design suits the native landscape. Larger rocks would not complement the setting. The river rock, laid over two thicknesses of landscape fabric, requires periodic weeding. Otherwise the labyrinth needs only mowing and trimming.

Visitors to this Carolina Low Country garden can rest in the shade of this rustic, vine-clad pergola after following the paths beyond. The pergola looks over the pleasing curves of the labyrinth.

Simple cut stone steppers lead the way to the labyrinth. The simple stone water bowl sunk into the ground along the path is an oasis for winged visitors.

2 Steps and Stairs

Stone steps and staircases serve as hardworking problem solvers in the landscape. As an integral part of a path, they allow you to traverse a slope. On a small incline, a few casual steps frame a passageway between garden rooms. More formal and essential, a careful staircase leads visitors safely up a hill to a front door. Either way, steps and staircases prevent erosion. They also provide entryways to other landscape features such as a raised patio or pool deck.

Flat stone steps (set randomly or less than uniformly) or stairs (made of three or more uniform steps) enhance any landscape by adding some excitement through variation as well as the drama of a strong focal point. Multiple steps and staircases add geometric order to the landscape with their horizontal forms.

Steps in the Landscape

Steps are useful tools to define a grade change and make a slope easier to climb. In a minimal way, a few broad stepping-stones cut into a gentle slope create a sense of transition. On a grander scale, a formal cut stone staircase provides a safe and sure way to climb a hill, say from the street to the front door of your house.

From a practical standpoint, steps connect levels and help make the trip more enjoyable. Besides providing a place to sit and chat with neighbors or to set containers of cheerful plants, steps show visitors that a landscape is well planned and improved. They bring order and structure to a landscape and may help define garden rooms. They are settings for wonderful vistas. A landing between flights of steps provides an opportunity for lingerers to enjoy potted plants, a bench, art, or a view.

If you find yourself leaning forward noticeably as you walk up a pathway or putting most of your weight on your toes and the balls of your feet—you are probably on a slope of 10 degrees or more—steps are needed. Sometimes steps are not required, but they provide a visual asset in the landscape that could not be gained otherwise.

Nine steps, gently curved, descend a 5-foot drop between the back door and a patio cut into the sloping site. The mortared stone steps echo the patio's construction materials.

Striking a balance between a rustic log house and its wooded mountainside surroundings, native Appalachian limestone forms a harmonious staircase that leads to the home's front entry. Coordinating light fixtures make the stairs more visible and safer at night.

Stone slabs shape deep steps that link areas of the landscape. Plants grow alongside the stepped pattern, providing lively counterpoints to the stones' rugged beauty and hefty sense of permanence.

A carefully cut and stacked red sandstone staircase issues an unspoken invitation to visitors: "Please direct your attention to this part of the garden." Fine thyme creeps between the stones and helps pave a fragrant path.

Designing Steps

Incorporate steps into any pathway with a slope greater than 10 degrees. For a relatively short pathway, you may need only a few gradual steps—short risers with deep treads work best. Steps leading to a house should be at least 3½ feet wide, preferably wider. A step connected to a landing provides a gentle way of breaking up a slope. A landing can be a large, flat slab of stone or a combination of flagstones or other flat pieces.

To climb steep slopes—more than 10 percent grade or 12 inches of rise per foot—plan a staircase with landings at least 30 inches deep. If you slope each landing a bit, the climb will feel more gentle and you may be able to reduce the overall number of steps.

When planning steps, determine the total rise (the vertical distance from the base of the steps to the top step) and total run (the horizontal length from the front edge of the bottom step to the back edge of the top step, not including any landing). Measuring the rise and run helps determine the dimensions for your steps. Determining this measurement is challenging when the steps are to be built into a hillside; estimate the rise and run and be prepared to make adjustments as you build.

Now you can determine the tread and riser dimensions: Twice the height of the step plus the tread depth should equal 25 to 27. This usually works out to a tread depth of 13 to 15 inches for a standard 6-inch rise.

Several broad steps, made with flagstone treads and wallstone edges, establish a threshold to an inviting garden room.

ADD INTRIGUE

Curving steps add a graceful element to a landscape. But when steps rise and vanish around the bend, the effect is more dramatic and intriguing.

Recycled sections of granite curbing are built into a retaining wall to create a stile. Stiles were once common in pastures—these staircases led people over a fence or wall while keeping sheep and cows at bay.

Selecting Stone for Steps

The largest, thickest, and flattest stones typically make the most stable steps. A single tread shaped from a mass of stone certainly has impressive appeal. But smaller flat pieces of stone can be mortared together to form handsome and durable steps.

Ready-made slab steps are among the most expensive stone products available. Cut or split 4 to 8 inches thick in widths suitable for staircases, the massive slabs of limestone, bluestone, sandstone, and granite are also available in random widths.

More economical options include stacking broad slabs of cut wall stone or laying large pieces of flagstone to form steps. As another alternative, steps can be constructed of concrete and topped with a stone veneer.

When choosing stone, look to other prominant landscape elements for inspiration. If your yard features a stone patio or stone wall, perhaps the same type of stone can be used to build stairs.

DON'T SLIP

Treads made of coarse-textured stone, such as sandstone, offer built-in traction that helps prevent accidents, especially when wet. Otherwise, traction can be sandblasted or cut into stone. A railing also adds valuable support. Lighting makes steps safer at night and highlights a staircase as a landscape feature.

Deep steps gracefully wind through this sloped, narrow backyard garden. The stepped pathway begins at a patio and skirts herb, vegetable, and perennial gardens before terminating at a sitting area.

Steps provide a stage for container plantings, allowing potted plants to be featured on each level. Pots are best set off to the side of wide steps where they will highlight the walk up or down without interfering.

Stone has a starring role in this thoughtful landscape redesign that turned a weedy, eroding slope into a grand entryway. Neatly cut and mortared steps contrast with an adjoining fieldstone retaining wall.

BUILD A MORTARED STAIRCASE

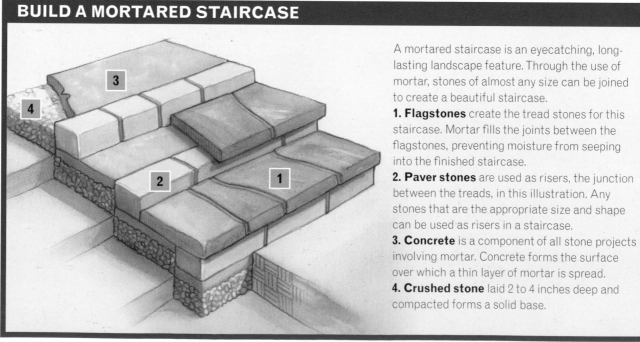

A mortared staircase is an eyecatching, long-lasting landscape feature. Through the use of mortar, stones of almost any size can be joined to create a beautiful staircase.

1. Flagstones create the tread stones for this staircase. Mortar fills the joints between the flagstones, preventing moisture from seeping into the finished staircase.

2. Paver stones are used as risers, the junction between the treads, in this illustration. Any stones that are the appropriate size and shape can be used as risers in a staircase.

3. Concrete is a component of all stone projects involving mortar. Concrete forms the surface over which a thin layer of mortar is spread.

4. Crushed stone laid 2 to 4 inches deep and compacted forms a solid base.

Building Steps

It takes careful planning and considerable skill to build stone steps and stairs that are solid, attractive, and safe. Accurately measuring to calculate the steps' dimensions is crucial to the project's success.

After you complete your preliminary calculations, adjust the rise and run of your steps to make sure they're even, safe, and comfortable. The rise from one step to another must be consistent wherever you place two or more steps. People expect the height of each step to be consistent. Varying the height between steps more than 3/4 inch can cause stumbling.

Building steps or stairs requires additional attention to details. The site should be prepared as you would when making a path: Excavate the area and install base materials. Compacted crushed stone covered with a thin layer of sand provides a stable base for support and drainage of stone steps. Mortared steps call for a concrete base, whether preformed or built from scratch.

Prevent the adjoining slope from eroding and washing soil over the steps by planting it, setting additional stones in it, or building retaining walls.

Additional stone slabs along the stone steps help hold the slope while serving as platforms for a display of urns and flowering plants.

Landscape Visit: Pebble Perfection

Cracked concrete steps and a crumbling walkway presented an opportunity for decorative stonework at the front entry of a 92-year-old home in Portland, Oregon. The new stone hardscape, designed to set the stage for the Craftsman-style house, works in a charming, handcrafted manner. The mortared stone also minimizes maintenance.

The steps, walk, and walls, constructed with a complementary mix of materials, blend together and form an inviting entryway. Flat slabs of Pennsylvania bluestone provide even footing as the walk steps up to the front porch stairs. Smooth, round fieldstones set on a 6-inch base of crushed stone integrate the garden walls and step risers into the design. The random placement of the stones is reminiscent of nature and is offset with artfully composed pebble mosaics.

A project like this one presents opportunities to incorporate stone of all shapes and sizes into the landscape. Create a cohesive look by repeating materials and elements.

Pebble mosaics garnish the bluestone walkway with colorful veins and spirals.

(Right) In the often-wet Portland climate, the character of the stones used in this design becomes more apparent.

(Below right) Colorful stonework creates a dramatic effect where curved stone walls and adjacent pebble mosaics sweep toward the front steps.

(Below left) The unique colors and textures of the stones are highlighted in this simple stone light fixture base, a perfect complement to the nearby mosaic stairway. Mortar holds the stones and pebbles in place.

3 Patios

A well-planned patio provides much more than a floor for furniture or a stepping-stone between house and yard. Aim for an outdoor room that makes the best use of the site and serves your household's needs. As an extension of your home's living space, a patio should be versatile and provide room for relaxing, dining, entertaining, playing, and other similar activities that you enjoy outdoors. When you use stone to make a beautiful and inviting outdoor room, you'll enjoy its season-to-season practicality with little maintenance.

Patio Ideas for Outdoor Living

What do you want your outdoor room to do? Ponder this question and begin the planning process by making a list of all the ways you could use your patio. As you dream of possibilities, note how the following factors affect the scheme of things: How does traffic flow between house and yard, with the patio as a transition or a separate area? What would you view from the patio? How would sun, shade, wind, and other weather factors affect your use of the area? Is there a place for storage with easy access and what would you keep there? How do you use adjacent areas and how would this use affect the patio's design? Is there access to utilities?

As you begin to picture your dream patio, considering all the limitations and possibilities of your site, keep in mind that many of the ideas shown on the following pages may be adapted to a terrace (on a slope) or a courtyard (an enclosed area). Most often, a patio sits at the back of the house and provides a lovely outdoor dining area within easy reach of the kitchen. A room that has many functions and offers privacy and shelter from weather would be ideal. Once you define your patio's location and purpose, you're well on the way to achieving the dream.

Focus on practical aspects, then fit amenities into the scheme, depending on your budget. A stone patio offers durability beyond your lifetime with the payoffs of increased home value as well as outdoor-living pleasure.

A bluestone patio extends the entertaining space beyond the walls of this home. As an outdoor floor, a patio effectively ties the house and yard visually and functionally.

Large cut stone slabs create an illusion of space in this small, confined area. Laid in a regular pattern and delineated by moss, the floor conveys orderliness.

Sealed stone provides a wash-and-wear patio floor that stands up to heavy use.

A flagstone floor works flawlessly with stone-veneer cupboards in this outdoor kitchen that services year-round enjoyment for entertaining and meal preparation.

This faux-flagstone patio is made of colored and stamped concrete—an inexpensive way to get the look of stone. The textured surface proves slip-resistant—perfect for an outdoor living area next to a pool.

Cooking Alfresco in an Outdoor Kitchen

Incorporating an outdoor kitchen into your patio plans entails additional thought and perhaps minor modifications. Whether you want a modest grilling island within steps of the house or a fabulous freestanding resort-style room, an outdoor kitchen allows you to cook, eat, and clean up without running in and out of the house.

Start with an appropriate floor, retrofitting a patio for your outdoor kitchen or installing flooring to go with any design style. With your budget and design needs in mind, match style and stone options. Typical choices are contemporary slate; Tuscan-look tumbled pavers, travertine, or exposed aggregate; traditional dark flagstones or cobblestones; and tropical stonelook concrete. The floor should be even and slip-resistant, ready to handle heavy foot traffic. Consider applying a penetrating sealer to protect the floor from food and drink stains and make it even easier to clean and maintain.

Your outdoor kitchen will be equipped for year-round use and convenience if it features a roof, built-in appliances, and utilities (gas, electric, and water). A countertop can double as a bar and breakfast table. Weatherproof storage keeps cooking and serving utensils dry and handy. Using stone for the room's surfaces—floor, walls, columns, countertops—gives the place durable and lasting qualities. When the materials repeat in the surrounding landscape, continuity occurs.

A mortared flagstone patio forms a solid platform for this well-equipped outdoor kitchen. For a cohesive look, take cues from the patio and incorporate mortared flagstone into entryways and paths.

Dine in the Garden

Where there's a patio, alfresco meals are sure to happen. You need no more than a table and chairs to outfit the place in simple or elegant style. Whether you begin or end the day in your outdoor dining room, you will find that mealtime takes on a fresh dimension when it's accompanied by birdsong or glimmering starlight.

Keep in mind these parameters as you plan a patio for dining: Stone—especially cut stone, pavers, and flags—provides a level, easy-care floor. An 8×10-foot patio would suffice for a family of five, including a 48-inch round table (which takes up less space than a rectangular one). To leave room for movement around the area, allow 36 inches between table edge and wall. Place a table at least 60 inches away from stairs.

Locate your outdoor dining room as close to the kitchen as possible for convenience. Allow enough room for the types of meals you enjoy most—whether intimate family dinners or lavish parties. Sited on the south or west side of your residence, you'll be situated for late-day sun and sunset. Take in the rising sun and enjoy evening shade when dining on a patio on the east side of your house.

When you're relaxing on your patio, you'll want to feel a sense of privacy. If the site doesn't provide enclosure with walls, fences, or plantings, consider how you can enhance it. Without a natural canopy of trees, a protective ceiling comes with an added overhead structure, such as a pergola, arbor, or awning. When you add a wall or fence to boost privacy, it will also help tie the patio to the landscape. Depending on how exposed the patio is to neighbors or passersby, a low wall or latticework fencing may be all that's needed to help define the space and create privacy.

Mortared flagstone makes it easy to shift dining chairs over this patio surface. In addition to mortared stove surfaces, cut stones create a smooth patio floor.

Limestone flags, sourced from a nearby quarry, give this Texas Hill Country patio a timeless feel. The stone-veneer pillars support a vine-covered pergola that provides welcome shade.

Red Colorado flagstone unifies the design of this backyard that features a dining patio (cut flagstone), a pond (boulders and slabs), and a wall (stone veneer).

A seaside terrace intended for entertaining shows off cut bluestone for an attractive floor that withstands continuous exposure to salt and sand.

Slate tiles cover a courtyard floor, giving it indoor styling and banquet comfort. The soothing colors help set the mood of the relaxing setting.

Retreating to the Patio

Outdoor rooms expand your comfort zone by giving you a place to retreat to in solitude, relax with a special someone, or gather with an intimate group of family or friends. Complete with minimal furniture, this place will enable you to steal away and daydream or sip drinks while visiting.

Outdoor sitting areas are often located in a garden, where there's just enough space for a couple of chaise lounges or benches. Away from the household's daily bustle, your retreat might be situated at the end of a path, secluded among trees, or tucked into a quiet corner. Alternatively you might find a spot for a patio off your master bedroom or home office, where it's most likely to offer convenience and comfort.

Wherever the location, an intimate gathering space should settle into the site rather than impose itself on it. Stone makes an ideal surface for this type of area because it defines the space and blends it with the surroundings. Gravel or flagstone works well for casual settings.

Patios typically get the most use in the evening, so include lighting to extend your use of the place by making it safer at night. Path lighting will make the flooring visible. You don't need to illuminate the entire floor for safety, but make steps or stairs clearly visible. Otherwise use lighting to create ambience, keeping fixtures above or below eye level for best results.

A casual outdoor sitting area calls for a rustic floor. Native flagstone, set in sand, blends with the surroundings.

Wrapping a Pool in Cool Stone

In the realm of backyard retreats, few scenarios can surpass the beauty and allure of a swimming pool—especially one surrounded by a stunning stone patio. Also called pool decking, this paved surface adds useable space to an outdoor living area, providing a transition between pool and house as well as room for lounging, strolling, and socializing.

Safety is of utmost importance when planning a pool deck. Choose stone that is not slippery when wet and remains cool underfoot. Sandstone, with its natural slip resistance, is widely used. Light-color stone such as white limestone and pale gray slate are popular as heat-reflective surfaces. A pool or spa makes a big splash next to a patio—literally as well as visually—so work with a reputable stone supplier who will guarantee that the stone you choose can resist the effects of the pool or spa chemicals.

Stone paving around a pool should drain away from the pool's edge and be easy to clean or hose down. Mortared or tightly set stone minimizes the presence of sand, dirt, and other grit that can get into the pool. The pool deck must be designed to stand up to the vagaries of the extreme weather conditions in your region.

Stone is also a popular pool coping material, set at the pool's waterline, merging the water feature and the surrounding patio in a natural-looking way. Boulders and fieldstones can also be set at the water's edge for an always-been-there look. Rustic stones are an essential part of a poolside waterfall.

Arizona sandstone adds flair to this poolside setting. The combination of flagstone and boulders enhances the natural feel.

COOL UNDERFOOT

Choose swimming pool decking that won't get too hot for bare feet. Light-color stone pavers or flagstones stay cooler than dark slabs of stone or concrete. Heat dissipates more quickly between smaller pavers.

(Right) While a swimming pool adds to a relaxing backyard retreat, the choice of rough flagstone for the decking contributes to its lagoonlike look and feel.

(Below right) Cool-on-the-feet limestone flags are paired with limestone boulders to wrap the pool and spa in stony style.

(Below left) Red flagstone pavers, with their random shapes and joints of creeping mint, complement the home's Spanish style.

Choosing a Site for Your Patio

Determining the best location for a patio depends on your property. As you consider the possibilities, ask yourself: How and where would a patio fit into the overall setting as it relates to the house and surrounding landscape?

Most often, a patio fits into an area at the back of the house, providing a lovely outdoor dining area within easy reach of the kitchen. As a transition from the garden to the house or between the house and the garage, the patio attractively links the structures with the landscape and helps make distant garden areas accessible.

Before you settle on the location, size, and configuration of your patio, consider any overlooked areas of your yard that may go largely unused. Situated in a spot away from the house, secluded from nearby traffic and neighbors, a patio located there could be perfect for unwinding at day's end. A front yard patio might open the entryway to your home and provide room for flowerbeds.

When designed to the scale of the setting, your patio's size will complement the site proportionately, making it more useful and enjoyable. When space is limited, make sure the patio site can provide the features you want most, such as a dining table and chairs, along with appropriate space so diners are not cramped. A large lot typically accommodates more options—distinct areas for entertaining and playing, room for adults and kids to gather simultaneously and separately.

Although most patios are square or rectangular, would a rounded design make better use of your space? It might surround a tree, emphasizing its shape and taking advantage of the shade, for example. A patio that wraps around a corner of the house might be accessible from several rooms and have greater potential use.

SOLUTIONS FOR SMALL SPACES

Make a small space seem larger using these tricks that also enhance a sense of seclusion and comfort.

- Create one large area from two smaller ones. For example, let the patio spill out into the yard.
- Draw attention to the patio instead of its perimeter or nearby property lines by blurring the boundaries with planting beds.
- Borrow nearby views, whenever possible. Instead of walling off the patio entirely, leave the view open to the neighbors' trees and shrubs, blocking only distracting views or screening strategically to enhance privacy.
- Use spacesaving built-in seating and a round table.

This island patio paved with Sydney Peake flagstone harmonizes with the stained stucco fireplace. The stone, chosen for its gray and rust hues, is used in paths and walkways throughout the landscape.

A large bluestone patio and massive fireplace suit the scale of this two-story suburban home. Split Tennessee-fieldstone veneer covers the fireplace and low wall and helps meld the outdoor room with its wooded background.

In the absence of a backyard, a narrow side yard can easily become a patio. Located just outside the kitchen, the flagstone patio is a charming outdoor dining room.

Carved into a shaded corner, this casual flagstone patio provides a quiet place for conversation and refreshments.

Find the Perfect Patio Style

The best patio designs extend beyond function. You'll be most comfortable in the space and savor time spent there when its style appeals to you, reflects your personality, and complements your existing landscape.

Choose a style that marries your house and landscape, following a theme set by existing materials: Combine stone with brick in the patio for a traditional brick cottage, for example, then include the same stone in the gardens. Or your scheme could echo rustic surroundings with the rough surface and irregular shape of flagstone set randomly. Mortaring the stone would make the surface more complementary to a shingled house.

A mix of paving materials gives you more room for creativity and expressing eclectic tastes. A blend of light-color cut stone and beach pebbles could add subtle contrast to an unusual patio design.

Attain a formal or informal style through your choice of materials and the use of lines, shapes, and angles. A formal, geometric patio could be made with smooth, straight-cut granite, marble, limestone, or bluestone in a tight-fitting layout. At the most informal end of the spectrum, patio designs include gravel or irregular stones, curved lines and free-flowing shapes. Low-growing plants creep between the flagstones or pavers.

PLANT YOUR PATIO

Plants help bring a patio to life and blend it with the surrounding landscape. Tuck groundcovers and creeping plants into the gaps between pavers and allow them to fill in. Trim them back when they grow out of bounds.

Straight angles shaped by a cut stone terrace direct visitors to a secluded dining area. The concrete balustrade and other formal accents complement the stone.

Selecting Patio Materials

Selecting the materials for your patio is as satisfying as viewing the finished construction. Visit stone and landscape suppliers to see materials firsthand and get a sense of what appeals to you most. After considering a range of stone types, colors, textures, shapes, prices, and installation levels, narrow your choices to a few. Then bring home samples and look at them in the context of your home and landscape.

Your choice of materials will help the patio blend architectural aspects of the house with natural elements of the landscape. Sandstone unites the adobe look of many desert-style houses with the native environment. It also suits the weathered appearance of an established home and brings earthy warmth to pool decking.

Once you visualize how the texture and color of the patio will relate to the house and yard, decide if you want to include edging. It can help maintain the patio's shape or give it the finished look you seek. Framing a loose-stone patio with cobblestones or pavers, for example, helps keep the gravel from scattering into adjoining areas. Edging also creates a contrast between the patio and yard. Where lawn and patio meet, the edging should be placed at a mower-friendly height.

Choose the best flooring that your budget allows. The cost of a patio will include base materials, edging, and surface stone, plus delivery and handling. Select the look you want, then adjust your material selection if the initial plans become too expensive. Combine flagstone with less costly gravel to cut costs.

The quiet, walled courtyard of this Italianate-style home features limestone squares laid diagonally and set apart with river rock. The offset design helps create an illusion of greater space.

(Above) Cut stone with an uneven boundary blurs the lines between house and yard. The tightly set stone makes a refined floor that suits the European-style house.

(Above right) A change in flooring materials, such as a shift from square pavers to mortared flagstone, helps indicate a transition between outdoor rooms.

(Right) Concrete and stone pavers display different, complementary patterns—one also includes brick and gravel. Combining materials like this allows you to stretch your budget.

A simple pergola provides shade to extend the usefulness of this patio. When choosing flooring for an outdoor kitchen, choose stone that's extremely durable and easy to clean. It should be able to withstand frequent splashes from the sink, grill, prep area, dining table, and possibly a nearby pool.

Mortared stone pillars and walls topped with large pieces of cut stone create a lasting outdoor dining space.

Designing an Outdoor Kitchen

When your patio paves the way for an outdoor kitchen, additional planning will be necessary. Whether you designate the area primarily for cooking or dining, or want a complete facility that accommodates various activities and offers room for storage, it should be located conveniently. Easy access from the house and a direct traffic route for visitors are essential.

If the patio is connected to the house, it will be easier to install the necessary utility lines and to buffer the space from sun and wind. For added protection the roof can be extended over the area.

Situated away from the house, a freestanding outdoor kitchen often offers more design options and total area than a kitchen right outside the back door. A kitchen with built-in features and a pergola adds to the project cost, but the amenities will also extend the season for outdoor cooking and dining.

You'll discover endless options for outdoor kitchen design. The best strategy will include choosing a site that works with your home's floor plan, the topography of the yard, and your plans for using the kitchen. Similar to a home kitchen, a well-planned outdoor facility will be arranged to allow for prep work, cooking, serving, eating, and cleanup—much of it at the same time. The scheme will also allow people to move freely around the area as they work, eat, and interact.

Among the most popular outdoor kitchen features is a workspace that offers a prep area, grill with side burners, and a sink. This outdoor kitchen also includes storage areas.

Enhance Your Outdoor Room

Comfort is key to any patio design. Your plans for using the patio will help determine whether it offers overhead protection from the elements or has supplemental heating. Features that address cooling and heating will help make the area comfortable and extend the use of the patio to a year-round outdoor room. In addition, an overhead structure increases privacy.

The usual ceiling of sky, while beautiful and expansive, is not always the most practical for a patio. An area intended for hosting large parties and kids' play benefits when left open to starlight and open air. Intimate areas planned for dining, conversing, and relaxing feel more inviting and cozier with an overhead feature, such as a pergola, arbor, lanai, or canopy. Shelter at least one-third of the patio for best results. In hot climates, consider covering the entire patio for optimum comfort.

An overhead structure provides shelter from sun, rain, and wind. It's likely you'll want to soak up a few rays and then retreat to cool shade on your patio. So you'll want an overhead designed to provide for both scenarios. The best physical protection comes from a solid roof. Louvers or latticework, combined with plants or not, allow varying amounts of sun and shade.

After sunset, especially during chilly times of the year, a toasty fire adds instant warmth and coziness. Include a fireplace, fire pit, or portable fire source, such as a chiminea, to your patio plans and enjoy the pleasures of a little fire—the sight, sound, aroma, and magical mood it creates.

A ceiling fan, outdoor speakers, and lighting enhance the comfort level of this patio. For simple installation, integrate these features when the patio is constructed.

In regions where the climate limits outdoor living, a fire pit extends the seasons by taking the chill out of spring and fall evenings.

BUILD A FIRE PIT

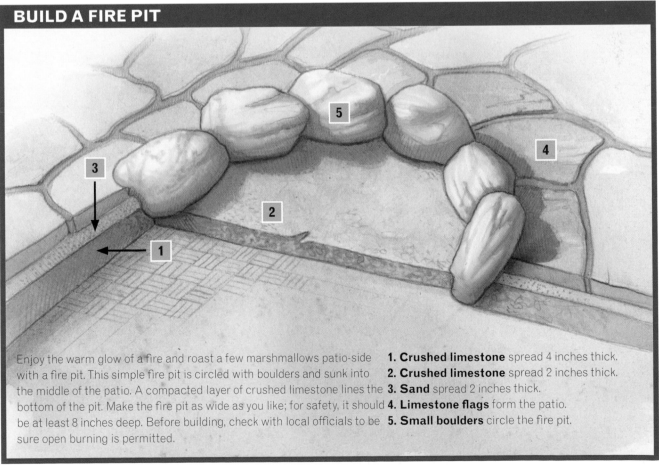

Enjoy the warm glow of a fire and roast a few marshmallows patio-side with a fire pit. This simple fire pit is circled with boulders and sunk into the middle of the patio. A compacted layer of crushed limestone lines the bottom of the pit. Make the fire pit as wide as you like; for safety, it should be at least 8 inches deep. Before building, check with local officials to be sure open burning is permitted.

1. **Crushed limestone** spread 4 inches thick.
2. **Crushed limestone** spread 2 inches thick.
3. **Sand** spread 2 inches thick.
4. **Limestone flags** form the patio.
5. **Small boulders** circle the fire pit.

DRAIN A PATIO

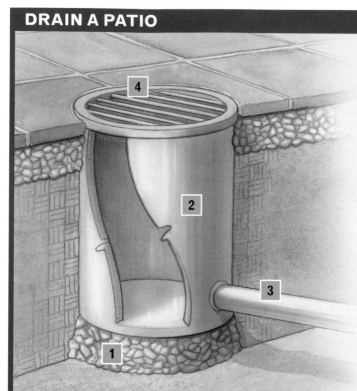

Where there are water runoff or drainage issues that cannot be amended by grading, an underground drainage system can help. Before you begin a landscaping project such as constructing a patio, plan and install any needed drainage to prevent runoff and water damage. Figure out the route—including the exit—for a drainpipe. Use gravity and direct runoff downhill whenever possible. Use solid rather than perforated pipe when draining water away from the house.

A catch basin is a drainage device built into a patio. This open surface drain has a receptacle that holds water and disperses it through the drainpipe when it reaches a certain level. Position a catch basin at the lowest point of the patio so the patio surface runoff drains toward it.

1. 4-inch gravel base

2. Catch basin is available at garden center or home-improvement store.

3. Drainpipe slopes to a distant dry well or, if codes permit, the storm-water drainage system.

4. Basin cover is integrated into the patio.

This cut bluestone patio transforms a mucky area of poorly draining soil into a source of constant enjoyment. Simple plantings around the patio's perimeter complete the shaded retreat.

Preparing a Patio Site

Your patio should be level and stable enough to support tables, chairs, and foot traffic. Careful planning will help ensure smooth, safe transition areas, especially along edges and in corners.

At the same time, the patio should slope away from the house—1 inch per 10 running feet—so water will drain off readily and run toward lower ground. Moisture will not soak down through a mortared stone patio. When the site is low lying and the soil contains clay, it may be prone to flooding. Ensure that adequate drainage is installed during the patio construction.

If a patio will be situated near a downspout, or if water puddles around a patio's perimeter, additional drainage is necessary. To remedy the situation extend the drainpipe from a downspout or excavate and lay a french drain to carry the water away.

Your primary goal will be to minimize any damage caused by improper drainage. Standing water and misdirected runoff may damage foundations, hardscape, or plantings. Identify runoff patterns in your landscape before grading any areas. Grading should be done before the patio is laid out and excavated.

Significant changes in grade on a sloping site call for terracing or steps. Use a slope to your advantage, where it can create privacy and shelter from wind. Level a slope by cutting into its side to remove soil and form a plateau, or fill in a low point, or do both to create a level surface for your patio. Build a retaining wall to hold a slope in place, if needed.

Wide-set flagstones easily accommodate a gently sloping site. A small water garden, ringed with fieldstones, is situated next to the patio for optimal enjoyment and easy maintenance.

Installing a Patio Base

Ensure the longevity of your patio and minimize repairs by following a few guidelines for constructing a substantial base. Once the site has been laid out, excavated, and firmly compacted, it's ready for the base installation.

The base for any patio should be level (while allowing for slope) and drain well. When properly laid, it will provide a stable yet flexible foundation for the paving. Patio and pathway construction are much the same—only the layout and purpose vary. It's especially crucial that adequate drainage provisions be made for a patio.

Before a truck arrives at your home with a load of gravel for the base, prepare the site to eliminate any hazards. Flag trees and surround them with brightly colored plastic fencing to help protect them from damage during construction. Mark heavy equipment access points. Barricade the driveway or other areas to protect surfaces.

For a dry-set patio, a base of crushed stone should be laid 4 to 6 inches deep and compacted. A deeper excavation allows for freeze-thaw action in cold climates, Zone 5 and colder. A 1- to 2-inch layer of sand tops the gravel and provides a level subbase for the paving.

Laid next to the foundation, this cut stone patio slopes slightly away from the house to promote adequate drainage. Even small patios require an adequate well-draining base.

BUILD A MORTARED FLAGSTONE PATIO

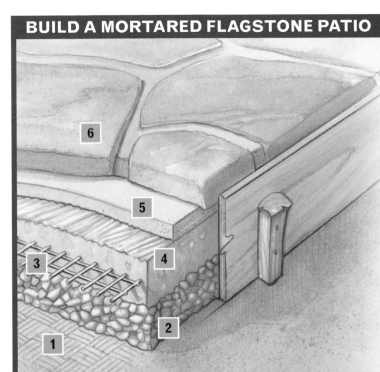

Mortar combined with a reinforced concrete slab adds longevity to a flagstone patio. A mortared patio excavation needs to be 10¾ to 12 inches deep (4-inch gravel base, 4-inch concrete pad, ¾- to 1-inch mortar bed and 2 to 3 inches of flagstone).

1. Soil is moistened and tamped after excavation to form a solid base.

2. A 4-inch gravel bed is compacted with a power tamper to form a solid base for the concrete.

3. Reinforcing wire mesh prevents the concrete slab from cracking (ask for 6×6 10/10 mesh).

4. The surface of a 4-inch layer of concrete is roughened with a scarifier or a notched trowel to help the mortar firmly adhere.

5. A ¾- to 1-inch layer of type-M mortar adheres the flags to the concrete.

6. Flagstones are set in place with mortar. Add or remove mortar as needed to level the flags. Fill the joints with additional mortar.

A mortared flagstone patio makes a rustic surface that complements the shingled house. Properly laid on a substantial base, a patio like this will better withstand the rigors of frigid weather cycles.

Finish Your Patio in Style

Flagstone, cut stone, or stone pavers can be set on sand or mortared to a concrete slab. The site layout is the same for both methods. For a solid, mortared surface, installation is similar, beginning with a 10- to 12-inch excavation and a 4-inch crushed stone base. A 4-inch concrete pad is poured over the gravel. Once the concrete has cured and developed its full strength (up to a week), the 2- to 3-inch layer of stone is mortared in place. Then wet or dry mortar can be used to fill 1/2 inch or smaller gaps between the stones.

If a gravel patio lies in your future, the installation process couldn't be simpler. Once the 6- to 8-inch-deep excavation is complete, edging such as stone pavers or cobblestones are set in place. A 4-inch base of crushed gravel is poured, covering the excavation, then compacted and topped with heavy-duty landscape fabric. A 2- to 4-inch layer of gravel completes your patio. Or follow the abbreviated steps in "Build a Quick Gravel Patio" to create a simple, though less durable, patio.

A gravel or dry-laid patio is the best choice for a site where the patio will be built around trees. Use the trees to your advantage, as they bring shade to the setting. Protect your trees: Avoid damaging their roots during landscape construction and lay the type of patio—gravel or dry-laid stone—that will allow moisture to reach the roots.

The base for this mixed material patio is the same as the base for a flagstone patio. Adjust the depth of the mortar to accommodate the thickness of the stones and brick.

Patterned after mosaics popular in Spain and Portugal,
this pebble patio features stone of various colors and sizes.

Build an informal patio like this one in an afternoon.
Simply sink stepping stones into the turf. Be sure the
stones are level with the surrounding soil for
easy mowing.

BUILD A QUICK GRAVEL PATIO

Make a gravel patio quickly on a small, level site using this simple method: Where there is turf, use a spade or square shovel to slice through the sod around the perimeter of the desired size and shape of the patio. Make the excavation approximately 3 inches deep. Remove the sod. Lay out heavy-duty weed barrier (landscape fabric) and install any desired edging. Spread gravel to fill the excavation.

Working with a Pro

You can save money by designing your patio, hauling the materials, and muscling the job. But enlisting the help of pros early in the process can save you time, extremely heavy work, and costly mistakes. If you are well informed about the project and its construction, you'll be able to manage the process.

Once you decide to contract some or all of the job, start gathering references for contractors. Ask friends and coworkers for their recommendations. Select prospective contractors, ask each one for a job reference, then contact them. Visit the job site, inspect the quality of craftsmanship, and inquire about the contractor's work.

Get several bids for the job. The bids of reputable contractors bidding for the same work should be comparable. Get all the specifics detailed in the contract: work to be done, materials to be used, start date, and completion schedule. Also find out about procedures for making changes, obtaining building permits and lien waivers, and resolving disputes. Your contractor should provide proof of licensing, bonding, and insurance.

An outdoor living area like this one that includes sophisticated features, such as a fireplace, pergola, and mortared patio, requires the planning skills of an architect or comparable professional.

TOP 5 QUESTIONS FOR YOUR CONTRACTOR

1. Will you provide a client's contact information for whom you did a comparable job?

2. What will the total cost be, including prices for materials?

3. What kind of a payment schedule can we negotiate?

4. When can you start and when will you finish?

5. Can you present a cost-plus contract? (This involves billing for time and materials, and sometimes a markup for overhead and profit. A fixed-bid contract may include an allowance for unforeseen problems or delays, which you will likely pay even if everything goes as planned.)

Retaining walls, a patio, steps, and even boulders are incorporated into this dreamy backyard retreat. A skilled landscape architect has the know-how to seamlessly interweave many outdoor amenities.

The stepped patio, gazebo, waterfall, and retaining walls at this location were constructed by skilled professionals.

This tiny urban patio is an intimate dining room with a captivating view. Cut slabs of Irish Linen limestone provide sure footing with lasting quality. Interspersed with flat black beach stones, the contrasting materials create striking interest.

Landscape Visit: Backyard Retreat

Picture a typical view outside the backdoor of a new urban townhome: Little but dirt and high wooden retaining walls can be seen. How could this miniscule space possibly become comfortable or usable, especially when the neighbors' windows look down on it? In this case, when the San Diego homeowners and their landscape architect saw the cramped barren space, they envisioned so many possibilities it was a challenge to keep the plan simple.

The homeowners wanted to eat, lounge, and entertain on their patio but opted to focus the design as a dining area. It took big thinking to consider every detail and carefully transform the tiny, empty pocket into an elegant outdoor room with contemporary flair and enough space for entertaining. The choice of stone as the primary landscaping material contributed in large part to the design's evolution and its success.

The couple wanted a low-maintenance area with privacy. A clever combination of stones and plants fit the bill. The existing wooden shoring wall was used to advantage. It became a raised planting bed when populated with easy-care plants, such as lantana, giant lilyturf, and rosemary.

Mulched and accented with fieldstones of various colors, the walled garden resembles a natural hillside. Tree ferns, bamboo, and ornamental grasses grow up rather than out over the patio and will mature into a living privacy screen.

Flat black beach stones fill the gaps between cut limestone pavers.

The 13×25-foot patio is a lush, private retreat with space for a table and chairs. The intimate outdoor room allows plenty of room for dining, entertaining, and lounging.

Landscape Visit (continued)

The key to this inviting, compact space is the patio's innovative design. As an indoor-outdoor room that's accessible from two bedrooms, the patio surface needed to be comfortable under bare feet. The homeowners visited many stone suppliers, and when they saw the soft, creamy color of Irish Linen, a variety of tumbled limestone, they had found their choice.

The cut limestone's straight edges and light color contrast with the smooth round river rocks that are scattered over the garden, forming a neatly unified effect. Between the limestone's irregular placement and a few broken corners, there are pockets in the flooring, casually filled with dark stones. Openings at the patio's perimeter leave room for a combination of stones and plantings.

One corner of this patio holds a small rock-lined pond and a trickling fountain. The water feature adds to the restful ambience of the setting.

(Above right) Tumbled blue river rock and small boulders hold back the hillside filled with low-maintenance plants.

(Above) Low-voltage lighting tucked among the stones and plantings accents the design and enhances its livability.

(Left) A solitary boulder stands as a captivating art piece. It forms an interesting transition between the patio's edge and the adjoining pond.

4 Walls

A stone wall stands in a home landscape as a serene focal point, drawing attention and inspiring a sense of calm. The enduring nature of a stone wall is captivating. A well-built stone wall can outlast several generations with little or no repair.

Walls take many forms and roles in the landscape, as you will soon see. Before you settle on a design, construction techniques, and materials, consider a range of possibilities for your yard and garden. In the end you'll likely join the legions of homeowners who have discovered that the value of a stone wall extends far beyond its cost.

Walls in the Landscape

Beyond their aesthetics, stone walls have always had functional value. They establish a boundary, especially along the border of a yard or a property line. While fences are usually built along lot lines, a stone wall might be more attractive and require little or no maintenance.

Within a landscape, freestanding walls delineate areas and define garden rooms. A counter-height wall might separate two areas that have related purposes, such as spaces intended for cooking and dining. The same wall's utility expands when it is topped with a flat surface perfect for a cocktail bar or breakfast counter.

The height of a wall helps define its purpose. A knee-high wall frames a lounging area or directs foot traffic; a thigh-high wall offers additional seating area. A 3- to 4-foot-high wall helps make a space more comfortable by shielding unsightly views, such as garbage cans, utility junctions, or a compost pile.

Higher freestanding walls—above 4 feet—form barriers, create privacy, and bolster security. When you need to separate your outdoor living space from neighbors' views or passing traffic, a high stone wall will do the job whether it encloses the area partially or completely. A solid wall helps keep kids and pets in the yard and unwanted visitors out.

A stone wall frames an outdoor kitchen and dining area. The openings in the wall act as doors, directing traffic in and out of the space.

Beyond its purpose of holding back earth, a hip-high retaining wall forms a planting area within easy reach—no stooping necessary when doing maintenance.

This dry-stacked wall is the perfect perch for a pair of flower-filled containers. Low walls like this are a simple way to delineate garden rooms.

(Above) Multihued flagstone is mortared together to create this durable wall. Sometimes a wall is the best way to divide an area of the landscape without interrupting the view.

(Above left) Several layers of dry-stacked wall stone form a raised bed that's ideal for a site with poorly draining soil. The raised bed is filled with a mix of topsoil and compost.

(Left) Rock-faced columns flank a driveway and support custom-designed lights. The river rocks adhere to a concrete core and are set in mortar.

Add Beauty with Walls

Walls create opportunities for beautifying the landscape, whether they form raised planting beds or serve as the backdrop for plantings. As a hardworking feature in your yard, a retaining wall holds a slope or grade change, keeping the earth from spilling out and preventing erosion. Sometimes, this type of wall forms a terrace, making an alluring place for relaxing and dining. When a retaining wall creates a raised planting bed, it enables you to garden without bending or stooping to the ground. Repeated in tiers, low garden walls create a terraced garden.

Picture a 3-foot-high stone wall along the front of your property line or where the yard borders a street, for example. Now imagine how that wall would look if it were set back at least 4 feet from the street and a colorful garden was planted in front of the structure—the effect becomes inviting rather than forbidding. Walls are intriguing landscape elements on their own, but when paired with plants they become beautiful landscape centerpieces.

As a backdrop for a garden, a wall often creates a nurturing microclimate for plants. The wall protects plants from wind and gives them the extra warmth needed to help them survive outside the limits of their usual hardiness range. This outcome depends on the direction of prevailing winds, regional climate, and plant selections. Consult a landscape professional or your county extension service when planning a walled planting area.

A curved wall partially encloses the patio, defining the space and integrity as an outdoor room for a guesthouse.

Designing Walls

The natural grace of a stone wall enhances any setting. What type of wall will work best in your landscape? Options include freestanding or earth-retaining, dry- or wet-laid (with mortar), and straight or curved. These choices, as well as the location, height, and length of your wall will determine its design.

Look around your community and see which wall styles, materials, and designs appeal most to you. Of course, the materials most readily available in your area and the potential cost of a wall's construction (considerably more than the stone itself) will affect its design.

The most rustic walls are dry-stacked fieldstone. Flagstone and cut wall stone create a more refined-looking dry-laid wall. Uniformly cut stone creates the neatest, most patterned effect suited to formal settings. Mortared walls also fit more tailored landscape designs. A mortared fieldstone wall appears more substantial than a dry-stacked one and it has more stability.

An unusual landscape feature, this gently arching bridge leads visitors over a small stream. It adds to the compelling nature of the path that wends through a strolling garden.

This informal wall is made of small boulders and a few flagstones mixed in here and there. The mix of stone shapes and sizes gives the wall a unique look.

A raised planting bed, made informally with dry-stacked limestone, suits a country or cottage garden. A freestanding wall like this serves a purpose more decorative than functional.

A classic limestone wall conveys a sense of permanence. Over time, as the stone weathers and plants grow up and over the wall, the structure develops more of a been-there-for-ages appearance.

ALL ABOUT WALL STONE

Stone Type	Color	Size	Ease of Use	Ideal Type of Wall	Cost
Fieldstone	Multicolored or assorted colors in a wide range	Softball-, football-, basketball-size	Least time and effort	Low, dry-laid; retaining	Economical
Cut wall stone	White to yellow, browns, grays	8 to 10 inches wide; 2 to 6 inches thick	Moderate time and effort	Any height, dry- or wet-laid; retaining	Varies by type; higher than most
Flagstone steppers	Quartz, limestone, sandstone, granite	10 to 20 inches across; 1 to 4 inches thick	Moderate time and effort	Any height, dry- or wet-laid; retaining	Varies by type; higher than most
Traprock	Gray to blue, gray, pinkish-gray	Boulders (100 to 500 pounds each)	Least time and effort	Low to medium, dry-laid; retaining	Moderate

Selecting Stone for Your Wall

The type of stone you select for building a wall plays a major role in the structure's finished appearance. When planning a wall, think about the possibilities of building with irregular rubble stone or cut and shaped ashlar. Rubble includes time-tumbled fieldstone and jagged traprock (rough-quarried granite). The latter locks together in a dry-laid wall with more stability than fieldstone. Ashlar includes wall stone—limestone and other rock—formed into random-length blocks. Flagstone steppers have become a popular wall-building material. Their somewhat flat surfaces and uniform thicknesses make them easy to stack and fit. They are commonly used to create low retaining walls.

Choose materials that complement your house and other landscape features, such as paths and patios. The stone's texture, shape, and color affects the wall's character. Thin slate or limestone forms a fine corrugated pattern, while granite boulders have a dense, heavy presence, for example. Rounded fieldstones can't help but exude casual charm. Traprock creates a rugged, multifaceted wall that resembles a wild rock pile and blends well with natural outcroppings.

Walls that include stones of various sizes look the most natural. This rough-cut wall stone has at least two flat sides that bolster tight and sturdy stacking.

Start with a Solid Foundation

Building a freestanding wall less than 3 feet high is a doable project for most people. A strong wall more than 3 feet high should be constructed by someone with the proper experience and training.

Any wall's integrity and stability come largely from its underground reinforcement structure. Once you've determined the best site for your wall, use stakes and string to mark its course. Then for a dry-laid wall less than 3 feet high, excavate 6 inches deep and twice as wide as the wall's thickness to prepare for a gravel foundation. To prevent shifting during freeze and thaw cycles, all mortared walls and dry-laid walls higher than 3 feet require a foundation that extends below the frost line. A mortared wall needs a concrete footing.

Before you proceed with the construction of a retaining wall or a freestanding wall in a poorly drained area, install a drainage system. Perforated drainpipe carries water away from the wall's foundation. Once the drainage system and gravel bed are laid, level and compact the foundation.

Without an adequate foundation and appropriate drainage, a wall may sag, crack, break, or collapse.

The foundation for a mortared serpentine wall like this is made the same way as a straight design. Lay out the shape by trailing flour across the yard or outline it with two garden hoses.

Wide slabs form a broadly curved retaining wall behind this pool. Strong enough to hold the sloping grade and upper terrace, it has a sophisticated look.

FOOTINGS

The foundation or footing of a dry-laid wall shifts with the ground as it freezes and thaws. As long as the wall is not cemented together, this isn't a problem. If the stones shift a bit over the years, you may need to refit one or two. A mortared wall, on the other hand, must rest solidly on a concrete footing for lasting stability.

Stacked flagstones circle raised beds in this herb and vegetable garden. Raised beds are back-friendly—less bending is required when tending these knee-high gardens.

Although the wall is only several years old, the natural weathering and irregular shapes of its Pennsylvania bluestone and old moss stone bring an instantly aged look to it.

BUILD A DRY-STACKED WALL

A well-built dry-stacked wall is art in the landscape. Patience and persistence are keys to creating a wall that stands tall and straight.

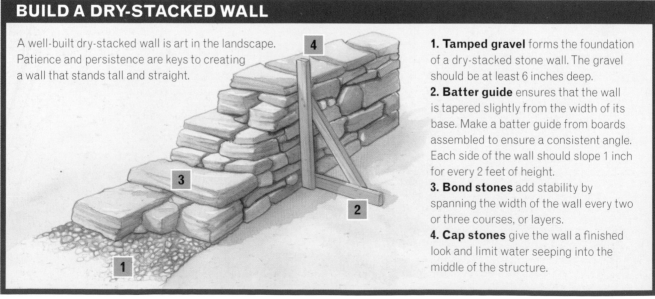

1. Tamped gravel forms the foundation of a dry-stacked stone wall. The gravel should be at least 6 inches deep.

2. Batter guide ensures that the wall is tapered slightly from the width of its base. Make a batter guide from boards assembled to ensure a consistent angle. Each side of the wall should slope 1 inch for every 2 feet of height.

3. Bond stones add stability by spanning the width of the wall every two or three courses, or layers.

4. Cap stones give the wall a finished look and limit water seeping into the middle of the structure.

Building Dry-Stacked Walls

The skill, time, and patience involved in creating a dry-laid, freestanding wall shows in its enduring beauty. This type of construction works with friction and gravity—the weight of each stone—to hold the wall together. The building process is comparable to doing a big jigsaw puzzle. It is painstaking and time-consuming because each stone must be set properly to fit tightly and rest solidly.

A well-made, tightly stacked wall has a strong and orderly appearance. The most secure walls include a combination of big stones and a variety of smaller ones.

Most likely, the stone for your wall will be delivered. Have it dumped in a place as close to the construction site as possible to minimize laborious lifting and carrying. If the stones sit on the lawn for an extended time, they may kill your grass. By the time the wall is completed, the surrounding lawn may need to be regraded and seeded.

A dry-stacked stone wall can be built of one stone type or several. As long as it rests on a firm base, the wall can move with the earth during freeze-thaw cycles in cold climates.

Building Dry-Stacked Walls

Make a dry-stacked wall as long as you like. The width at its base should be two-thirds of its height, with the sides tapering toward the top and giving the wall an inward, centralized balance. Walls more than 3 feet high require internal reinforcement and are best left to skilled builders.

For best results you'll need large, wide, flat stones for the bottom layer of the wall to give it stability—physically and visually. Various-size stones will be fitted like puzzle pieces for the wall's face, while small rubble can fill its center. Sort stones by size before beginning construction.

A well-built wall includes long bond stones—also called stretcher, tie, or through stones—that are placed at regular intervals about halfway up the wall. Placed widthwise, these stones tie together the two faces of the wall and give the structure more integrity.

As layers are added, the center of each stone should rest on the seam of the stones beneath it. The mantra of stone building—"one over two, two over one"—reminds you to stagger the joints.

Wide, flat capstones—the same kind or a different type of stone—form the top course of the wall, giving it a finished appearance. The capstones are typically mortared for stability, especially if the wall will be used as a bench.

The irregular New England fieldstones that frame this perennial garden were laid 2 feet wide to form a stable wall that stands up to rigorous weather.

Quarried stones, each with one especially flat side, top the wall with uniformity and give it a more formal look. Cut capstones would take the wall to the next level.

Layers of plants—from ankle-high sweet alyssum to towering delphinium—help tie this wall to the landscape and make it look more rooted to the earth.

Building a Mortared Wall

Freestanding mortared-stone and stone-veneered walls, constructed on poured-concrete footings, constitute permanent fixtures in the landscape. Although a mortared wall is inflexible, it gives you flexibility because it can be made narrower and built in a more limited space than a dry-laid wall.

A mortared wall also offers a wider variety of design options. The wall can be made of almost any kind of rock, a combination of rock, or a mix of rock and brick or concrete. What's more, various methods of applying and finishing mortar result in different joints, from hidden mortar that mimics the look of dry-laid stone to recessed, flush, raked, and beaded joints.

Veneered walls, made with ¾- to 1¾-inch-thick stone (called thin veneer) or 4- to 6-inch-thick stone (called thick veneer) mortared to a poured concrete or concrete-block core, can be made with real or artificial stones.

When building a mortared wall, begin with clean, dry stones. Dry-fit the first course, arranging the largest stones on the footing, then mortar them in place. Lay one or two courses per day, allowing the mortar to set and cure. Use a wet rag to remove any excess mortar from stones before it sets.

Stacked stone surrounds a circular fountain and the same type of stone was used to fashion the adjoining mortared wall. Mortared walls require built-in weep holes to facilitate drainage.

Mortar bonds these round fieldstones together, creating a 3-foot stone wall. The 5-foot cedar fence was added to keep deer from the enclosed garden.

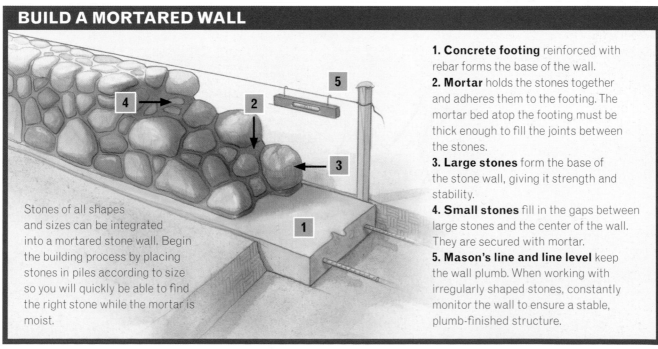

BUILD A MORTARED WALL

Stones of all shapes and sizes can be integrated into a mortared stone wall. Begin the building process by placing stones in piles according to size so you will quickly be able to find the right stone while the mortar is moist.

1. **Concrete footing** reinforced with rebar forms the base of the wall.

2. **Mortar** holds the stones together and adheres them to the footing. The mortar bed atop the footing must be thick enough to fill the joints between the stones.

3. **Large stones** form the base of the stone wall, giving it strength and stability.

4. **Small stones** fill in the gaps between large stones and the center of the wall. They are secured with mortar.

5. **Mason's line and line level** keep the wall plumb. When working with irregularly shaped stones, constantly monitor the wall to ensure a stable, plumb-finished structure.

The mortared steps built into a low retaining wall make a welcoming entryway to this backyard garden. The stonework extends into a mortared path.

BUILD A MORTARED RETAINING WALL

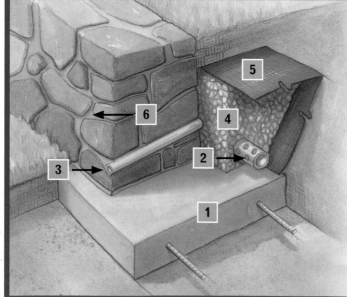

Mortared stone is the most permanent material to use for a retaining wall. Drainage is especially important in mortared retaining walls. Note the large and small drainpipes in this illustration.

1. Concrete footing creates a solid foundation for the wall.

2. Perforated large drainpipe collects most of the water cascading toward the wall. The pipe directs the water to a predetermined drainage area.

3. Weep hole from a small drainpipe lets excess water (water that is not collected in the large drainpipe) pass to the other side of the wall.

4. Gravel fill quickly ushers the water down to the large drainpipe.

5. Landscape fabric prevents soil sediments from seeping into the gravel and clogging the drainpipes.

6. Mortar holds the stones in place.

Adding Retaining Walls to the Landscape

A retaining wall holds back earth. While this goal is significant, it should not be the only design consideration. More important, a retaining wall must be designed to allow a passage for water to drain away from the wall. Hire a professional engineer or landscape contractor specializing in retaining walls to design and build a reliable wall more than 3 feet high.

Any number of retaining wall design options may be just what your landscape needs. For instance, a stone retaining wall that cuts into a slope frees space unsuitable for a patio or walkway. A wall that cuts into a level lawn and forms a sunken garden room creates a microclimate that extends the growing season. Or a series of low terraces can be used to create level playing fields in a once-sloped backyard.

As a major focal point in the landscape, a retaining wall should be attractive and suit the setting. Keep in mind that the overall size of the completed wall will affect the impact of its presence. A series of low terraces will work in much the same way as one massive retaining wall to tame a slope but will look completely different.

A wide range of stone works well for retaining walls, from hefty boulders holding back a hillside to distinctive stone veneer mortared to reliable concrete block. If you're interested in the look of stone but not its price, consider the options available with stone-look interlocking concrete blocks.

Squarish wall stones stack readily without mortar to make a substantial two-tier retaining wall that suits this country-style city lot.

Building Retaining Walls

Never underestimate the engineering required to build a retaining wall. The lay of the land and soil type have heavy bearing on a wall and must be considered. Building a low retaining wall to form a raised planting bed at the foot of a gentle slope is much different than building a 4-foot wall to hold back the cut left after excavating a driveway through a steep hill. You'll need professional advice and assistance, as well as a building permit, to build a retaining wall higher than 3 feet. A low wall can be accomplished by most do-it-yourselfers.

Any retaining wall includes a varied selection of stone sizes, with the most substantial ones at the base and smaller stones filling in behind the wall's face. A dry-stacked retaining wall must be built so that each course, or horizontal layer of stone, staggers backward into the slope. Staggering adds strength and will keep the wall from bowing or collapsing. The bank behind the wall should be cut away to angle back—bottom to top—minimizing any pressure it might place on the wall. Perforated drainpipe, laid in gravel behind the wall's base, will help carry water away. For stability, each course of the wall will be set back slightly so the wall angles back at least 6 inches for a 3-foot-high wall.

This retaining wall does double duty as steps. The terraced wall maintains a low profile and makes way for planting pockets at the top.

This curving wall, cut into a lakeside bank, required supreme built-in strength. As a solution, a hardworking concrete retaining wall is camouflaged by a veneer of mortared stone.

An 18-inch-tall wall retains soil in these garden beds while presenting an opportunity to create additional garden seating. Cut stone makes a smooth seat.

Accenting Walls

When designing a wall, look for opportunities to include practical elements such as lighting, seating, and planting. Any of these additions will make the wall more attractive and useful.

When lighting fixtures are incorporated into a wall located near an entryway or pathway, the effect enhances safety and security. The lighting fixtures you choose might extend from the stonework, creating dramatic effects at night, or they could tuck into recesses of the wall and be more subtle.

Plan ahead and consider a variety of other options that can be added to your wall when it is built. A neatly capped low wall can provide extensive seating—particularly useful near a patio. A bench, made from a wide stone slab, can be laid into the side of the wall.

In a home landscape, stone works with plants to compose a more natural-looking setting. Plants add color and lively character to a stone wall as they soften and help blend it into the landscape. Change a wall's appearance completely by draping it with trailing plantings, such as trailing rosemary. Gaps between stones in a dry-laid wall make ideal planting pockets for shallow-rooted plants, such as creeping varieties of sedum, phlox, and dianthus. A retaining wall that forms a planting area presents endless gardening possibilities, including perennials, flowering bulbs, shrubs, and more.

Succulent plants, such as *Sedum* and *Sempervivum* species, thrive in the crevices in this wall. The drought-tolerant perennials spread slowly.

PLANT YOUR WALL

Some plants are especially well suited to the usually extreme temperatures and tight conditions in the pockets of a dry-laid wall. These are a few that can be tucked successfully into gritty soil between the stones:

- Alpine pink (*Dianthus alpinus*)
- Basket-of-gold (*Aurinia saxatilis*)
- Candytuft (*Iberis sempervirens*)
- Fairy foxglove (*Erinus alpinus*)
- Fairy thimbles (*Campanula cochleariifolia*)
- Hen-and-chicks (*Sempervivum* spp.)
- Mountain avens (*Dryas octopetala*)
- Mountain sandwort (*Arenaria montana*)
- Silvery milfoil (*Achillea clavennae*)
- Stonecrop (*Sedum* spp.)

(Right) Creeping phlox and thyme grow in the crevices of this dry-stacked wall, softening the face of the structure.

(Below right) Built into the wall, this light casts a soft glow. Plan ahead when incorporating lighting into a wall, leaving access to wiring as needed for maintenance or repairs.

(Below left) An earthtone container creates a focal point atop the serpentine stone wall. Use the top of a stone wall for displaying containers or as additional garden seating.

Landscape Visit: Stony Update

Built in the mid-1950s on a small shady lot at the base of a steep hill, a modest home and its tired landscape needed more than an update. After 17 years in the coastal Southern California home, the homeowners decided on a complete landscape transformation.

　　With the help of a local landscape designer and a gardening class, they formulated a design to improve access to the house from the driveway, create more usable outdoor space, screen the driveway, add colorful low-maintenance plants, and wed the home to the landscape. Walls played major roles in achieving all of this and more.

The curving wall frames part of an adjoining patio where dining and relaxing are de rigueur. The stones' soft gray color, irregular shapes, and textures complement the natural flow of the landscape.

A complete landscape makeover using granite to create walls, paths, and a patio replaced the brick walkways and wooden stairs that once surrounded this Southern California home.

Mortared walls and cobblestone paths wind through this landscape. The mortar in the stacked-granite walls is recessed and less obvious than that in the walkway.

Landscape Visit (continued)

The first step in the landscape transformation was to excavate into the steep front bank to create room for a larger yard and then add a cobblestone path and patio. During the excavation, french drains were installed to divert water from the house and yard, preparing the way for more walls. A curving retaining wall holds the sloped front yard and helps break up the boxy shape of the split-level house. A similarly undulating stone wall separates and screens the driveway from the backyard.

Locally quarried cut and tumbled granite—one of the hardest and most durable of landscaping stones—forms the strong new walls for the hillside site. The wall stone has a soft gray color and a grainy, mineral-rich texture that complements the cobblestones used for the patio and paths. The cobbles, salvaged from Old San Francisco, also work with the wall stone to tie the freshly painted gray house to the landscape.

Ferns cascade over the granite wall, softening the stone's appearance. Foliage, rather than flowers, dominates this textural landscape.

Entry steps, shifted to the side of the yard during the landscape update, guide visitors to the improved pathway and the front door of the house. The walls' curves contrast with the steps' straight lines.

5 Edging

Decorative and functional, edging offers one of the easiest ways to enhance a landscape or garden design with stone. Although stone edging brings its natural and distinctive look to any setting, it can easily be designed to coordinate with your landscape style.

Typically used to facilitate the flow of one surface to another, edging works to blur or clarify boundaries. Use it to your advantage. Best of all, edging makes your life easier. Once it's installed, you won't need to edge garden areas for years to come. Edging laid as a mowing strip speeds this regular task and eliminates the need for trimming.

Edging in the Landscape

Properly installed edging is an efficient means of enhancing a landscape's design. Depending on the stone or other edging material you choose and how you use it, edging helps establish the garden's style, giving it a relaxed, casual look, an elegant feel, or whatever you desire.

Most commonly used to separate planting beds or paved areas from adjoining surfaces, edging adds the element of neatness to your landscape. When you use edging, a garden bed retains its shape. Soil stays in the bed and adjacent lawn is less likely to creep into the planting area.

Flat, round, sharp-edged, random-shape, dark, or light—these are some of the aesthetic qualities you'll want to consider when selecting edging. Your choice of edging material will affect the overall look of the pathway, patio, or other feature as well as the way it melds with the surrounding landscape. Fieldstone or wood edging would complement an informal walkway in a rustic setting, for example. Uniform cut-stone edgers laid end to end or a mortared edge makes a tidy statement with a more clearly defined sense of formal organization.

As you select an edging material, keep in mind how its color and texture will complement or contrast with any paving material it will edge. An edge of brick contrasts boldly with a surface of stone, while a concrete edge blends more harmoniously. Some types of metal or plastic edging do their job while having low—practically invisible—profiles.

Time-tumbled fieldstones grace the edge of a flowery cottage garden and repeat the curving flow of the picket fences.

Small, thin flagstones form an undulating boundary for this shaded perennial garden. The dry-stacked stones quickly shape an easy-care raised bed.

Stone is the primary design element in this Asian-influenced landscape. The edging stones and boulders coordinate to make a bold statement.

Dual edgings—casual fieldstones and tidy bricks—along this wide flagstone path manage to work well together because of the informal, cottage-garden context.

The height of edging affects the way it functions as well as its overall appearance. Set at ground level, this low-profile edge facilitates mowing.

Adding Stone Edging to the Landscape

You'll find plenty of opportunities to use stone edging in your landscape. When stone frames garden areas, it distinguishes them from the landscape as a whole and helps keep plants and soil within bounds. Edging a bed with large stones or stacking flat stones up to 18 inches high makes it possible to have a raised planting area. This is especially advantageous when the garden runs along a gentle slope—the edge helps keep the soil from washing away.

Areas paved with stone, such as paths and patios, may need some sort of substantial edging to keep them from dislodging or falling apart. In addition, any type of natural-looking pond, stream, or waterfall requires edging to hold and disguise its liner.

A gravel walkway or patio usually requires edging to help keep the loose fill from migrating into an adjoining lawn, garden, or other area. Where gravel or another stone paving material meets lawn, edging set close to ground level provides a mowing strip (a level surface used to guide a lawn mower's wheels while mowing the lawn's edge).

Edging steps or stairs with a cascade of fieldstones, for example, creates a naturally finished look. Adding stone details to the edge of a parking area—whether concrete, asphalt, or gravel—will boost the charm factor without breaking your budget.

Keep this in mind as you plan and add edging: Whether edging is set flush with the ground or raised, it can take a straight or curved course. The length of an edger affects the shape of a curve. It's easier to lay smooth curves with shorter edgers and straight lines with longer edgers.

The garden island, set in the midst of a flagstone patio, gets some of its formal structure from its edging—straight-sided flagstone set on end.

Selecting Stone Edging

Stone ranks high among the choices of landscape edging materials that offer natural beauty and rugged practicality. You'll find a vast selection of potential edging materials in the realm of stone. When you visit a local stone supplier, consider the possibilities in terms of their pros and cons.

Among the most likely candidates for edging, you'll find cut stone and pavers that can be set tightly together to form a uniform, elegant edge. Easily mortared and ideal as a mowing strip, these options are handsome but pricey. Ashlar—cut only on two sides—also creates a formal look but at a more moderate price.

Fieldstone suits cottage-style gardens and informal mixed borders. This economical option has wide color variations. Cobblestones, flat river rocks, or small flagstones work especially well as an aesthetically pleasing edge for a path. They are also well suited to a cottage-style or informal garden.

Other hardworking edging materials include concrete, pressure-treated lumber, composite landscape timbers, and brick. Place any of these around the perimeter of a path, patio, or planting area and watch them withstand foot traffic, wheels of gardening equipment, and weather. Plastic- and metal-strip edging, widely used between lawns and planting areas, work well for curves. Although cheap and easy, plastic deteriorates and pops out of the ground.

Separate edgers are not always necessary. Some well-made dry-laid paths and patios edge themselves. And plants provide color, contrast, and softness when no other path definition is needed along an edge.

Large fieldstones laid in a loose curve, harmonize with the informal plantings. Sweet alyssum adds a lacy touch.

The natural variations of shape and color help the stone ledge and the pool blend with the landscape.

Installing Stone Edging

Ideally edging for a path or patio will be installed after the base but before the stone surface is laid. For more details about how to edge a path, see pages 46–47, or water feature, see pages 160–161. Lay out any edge in advance of installing it, marking the excavation area with flour or powdered chalk. Use a garden hose as a guide when laying out a curved edge. Well-laid, long-lasting edging requires a drainable base of crushed gravel at least 2 inches deep.

You may choose an edging just because you like the way it looks. Choosing a high-quality material and ensuring that it is properly installed helps prevent repairs, replacements, and additional costs. When purchasing stone for edging, have a sketch of the landscape as well as measurements of the areas that will be edged with you when you visit a stone supplier.

Where it will serve as a mowing strip, stone or another edging material should be set no more than an inch above ground. If fieldstone or other stone edging sits well above ground, lay a band of gravel, mulch, or embedded stone between the lawn and stone edge of the garden bed to facilitate mowing.

Granite blocks form the raised beds of a formal vegetable garden. The hefty stones are set about 2 inches deep.

BUILD A RAISED BED

Jumbo granite cobblestones and pea gravel form the bones of a garden ripe with produce from spring to fall. Each of the beds is edged with 8×10×4-inch, larger-than-average cobblestones set in 2½-inch-deep trenches. Pea gravel covers the paths.

Begin building the garden by laying out the beds. The overall rectangle is 24×31 feet. The pea gravel paths are about 20 inches wide. Mark the excavation areas with flour or powdered chalk. Excavate and set the cobblestones. Fill the beds with quality topsoil and spread gravel over the paths.

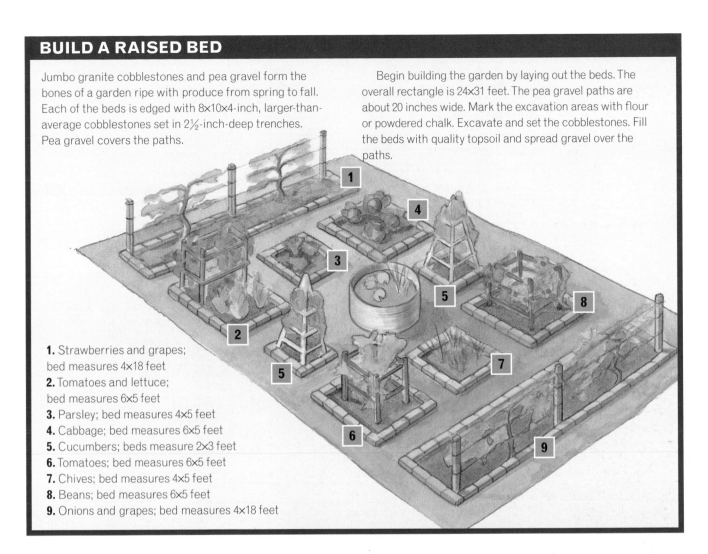

1. Strawberries and grapes; bed measures 4×18 feet
2. Tomatoes and lettuce; bed measures 6×5 feet
3. Parsley; bed measures 4×5 feet
4. Cabbage; bed measures 6×5 feet
5. Cucumbers; beds measure 2×3 feet
6. Tomatoes; bed measures 6×5 feet
7. Chives; bed measures 4×5 feet
8. Beans; bed measures 6×5 feet
9. Onions and grapes; bed measures 4×18 feet

Thick split stone has a rough texture that makes it ideal for stacking as a low wall.

The prairie wind that blows continually on this Canadian homestead has an extreme drying effect on plants and soil and makes gardening difficult. The living wall of spruce gives this garden the feel of a tranquil, secluded paradise.

The chartreuse Scotch moss between the flagstones spread from its beginnings in a 4-inch pot. Along with woolly thyme and pussytoes, the crevice plantings elbow weeds out of the pathway.

Landscape Visit: Wrapped in Flags

High atop a plateau on the Saskatoon prairie in Saskatchewan, Canada, the wind blows constantly. Gardening would be unlikely here without the sturdy wall of spruce trees planted on this windswept homestead 35 years ago. The evergreen shelterbelt effectively buffers the chilling and drying force of the gales and creates a cozy microclimate for an amazingly lush gardenscape.

A key component of the impressive shrub and perennial bed that sprawls across the farmyard is the wide flagstone path, edging the entire garden. The broadly sweeping curve of the path gives the landscape a dramatic sense of flow, from a swath of trees to the garden tapestry to the thick lawn. Made of flat fieldstones culled from the farm's fields, the path expands into rock garden areas here and there, where low-growing campanula, dianthus, heuchera,

and dwarf delphiniums thrive in the well-drained soil. The path also links two rock-edged ponds at opposite ends of the garden.

The massive flagstones at the garden's edge add to the protective microclimate by absorbing heat during the day and providing warmth to the nearby plants' root zones at night. At the same time, condensation forms beneath the stones, bringing moisture to the soil and plants. As a result, the stone helps plants survive extreme conditions of drought, wind, and other prevailing weather factors. Ground-hugging Scotch moss, woolly thyme, and pussytoes fill the crevices between the flagstones.

Groundcovers in between the edging stones have filled over several growing seasons, and perennials stand shoulder to shoulder in the border.

6

Water

The complementary qualities of water and stone—water's movement and transparency, stone's repose and solidity—create a satisfying effect that can improve almost any landscape. What's more, you can enhance the sound and the pleasure by incorporating stones that will cause water to splash, trickle, or swirl as it flows around them. Depending on the design, you can use a water feature to resolve a landscape problem, such as a boring or sloping site, turning it into a beautiful asset. A water feature gives you a way to transform your property—or part of it—into an environmentally friendly landscape that imitates a natural setting.

Features

Selecting a Water Feature

Landscaping with water and stone presents a wealth of design opportunities. A beautiful garden pool, a trickling waterfall, a rushing stream, or a glistening fountain—each of these possibilities offers aesthetic rewards, especially when combined with stone. The concept of the garden as a peaceful private sanctuary has inspired new interest in water features, although the pleasing accents have been incorporated into home landscapes for centuries. Who can resist a stroll around a pond and the hope of the gleam of a fish or the splash of a frog?

If your landscaping plans include a water feature, stone will help make it more realistic looking. Edged with stone, a new pond or stream acquires instant age, resembling a natural environment where dragonflies flit among irises.

As water falls into a pebble-lined stream and tumbles over a rocky ledge, it creates all the tranquillity you'd find in the wild—within steps of your door.

You may not have enough space in your yard for a mountain stream like the one you saw on vacation in the Rockies, but the wild one can still serve as inspiration. As you begin thinking about the design of a water feature, you'll want to consider how it will fit the site in terms of size, scale, and shape. Whether a full-scale watercourse or a small fountain suits your scheme of things, start by picturing a range of possibilities.

The pleasing sound from this waterfall enhances year-round enjoyment of the yard. A well-designed landscape that includes a water feature increases the value of the property as well as its aesthetic appeal.

Turn a landscape problem, such as an eroding slope, into a decorative asset by designing a water feature. The waterfall tumbling into a small pond adds aesthetic value.

A picturesque lily pond, adjoining a sun-dappled flagstone patio, transforms an ordinary suburban backyard into a spectacular setting. Large stone slabs bridge the pond and link the patio with the lawn beyond it.

When adding a pond to an established landscape, place the rocks so they appear to have tumbled into place, giving the feature a natural appearance.

Ponds in the Landscape

When constructing a pond, use stone in various ways, from accents to edging, covering the bottom, forming spillways, waterfalls, and streams. Rocks contribute to a pond's aesthetics as well as its function. For a natural-looking pond, large boulders work as accents, providing visual appeal in the pond and along its edge. Stones of varying sizes should be grouped with boulders and used to hold the pond's liner in place. Gravel fills between stones and behind boulders, adding stability to them and providing a habitat for beneficial organisms that you'll want to flourish in the pond. Beyond aesthetics, stone edging helps protect a pond's liner from the damaging effects of sunlight.

Stone helps integrate a well-designed pond into the landscape. Edging and accents of stone, set in a flat, sloping, mounded, or stacked manner, make the feature seem more settled and right for the site.

Proper placement of a pond is important. Before you choose a location, consider site conditions, including slope, soil, sun, shade, and wind. Also think about how you want to use the pond, the climate in your locale, and the location of utilities. Try to balance all these factors.

Your pond should suit the scale of the site—not too big to overwhelm an adjoining patio, for example, and not too small to seem like an afterthought or a mistake. A pond larger than 4×6 feet and at least 18 inches deep will be easier to maintain and keep ecologically balanced. Larger, deeper ponds accommodate more plants and fish. Backyard ponds can be installed in any size, shape, or configuration (with two or three levels, waterfalls, or a stream). Tuck a pond into a corner of your yard or build one that disappears under a deck.

Viewed from the front porch, this small circular pond features water lilies, flowering thalia, and goldfish. It offers entertainment value as it attracts birds, dragonflies, and other wildlife.

Edge Your Pond With Stone

Stone can help you create a landscape around a pond that's either realistic or fantastic. The stone you select for edging your pond should suit the overall look you want to achieve. Use indigenous rock for a natural-looking feature. Cut stone, flagstone, or pavers work best for edging a formal shape, especially one with a geometric design or mortared finish.

Select stone for edging your pond that complements other elements in the landscape. If you used fieldstone to edge walkways and planting beds, select stone with a similar shape, color, and texture to edge your water garden. Aim for harmony, not necessarily a perfect match. Choose one type of rock, such as granite, moss rock, or basalt, instead of a busy hodgepodge of different materials. Granite, basalt, and comparably hard rock are preferable to limestone because it (and softer rock) can crumble and release minerals into the water, upsetting the ecology. Stones that have at least one flat side will sit flush on the edge, providing a stable surface on which to stand or kneel. Rounded stones are more likely to roll into the water.

In order to make your pond as visually appealing as possible, follow a few guidelines. Incorporate water features and place each stone so it looks as if it belongs there. Instead of plopping a pond in the middle of a flat lawn and circling it with rock, mimic nature: Site the pond on a slope when possible and give it a believable context. Group stones of various sizes in the water at the edge of a quiet pond—some submerged, others rising above the surface.

The edge should be constructed to slope away from the pond, to help keep stones, other edging materials, and soil from washing into the water. Large boulders placed in a pond or at its edge require the extra support of a concrete pad, topped with an underlayment of old carpet to prevent damage to the pond liner. Edging stones should overhang the water 1 to 2 inches to do an effective job.

This pond appears to flow beneath the home as if fed by a hidden spring. Stone edging enhances the illusion by hiding the pond liner.

A viewing deck nestles in the shade close enough to the pond's edge to allow easy viewing as fish swim through the water.

Stones of all sizes—from pebbles to boulders—edge this pond, giving it a natural look. Smooth stones are especially suitable for their waterworn appearance.

BUILD A POND

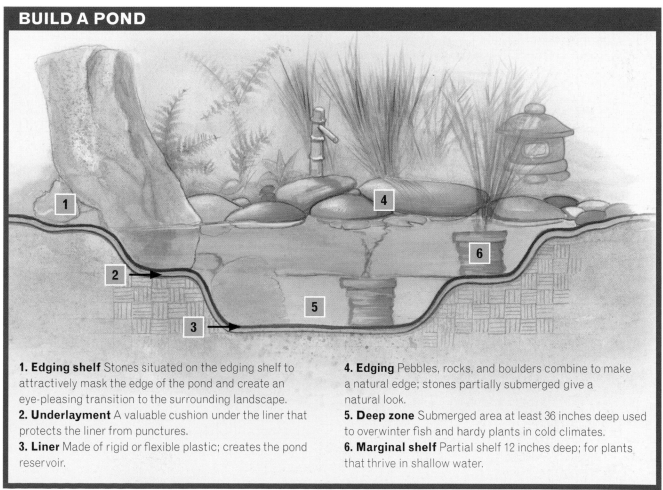

1. Edging shelf Stones situated on the edging shelf to attractively mask the edge of the pond and create an eye-pleasing transition to the surrounding landscape.

2. Underlayment A valuable cushion under the liner that protects the liner from punctures.

3. Liner Made of rigid or flexible plastic; creates the pond reservoir.

4. Edging Pebbles, rocks, and boulders combine to make a natural edge; stones partially submerged give a natural look.

5. Deep zone Submerged area at least 36 inches deep used to overwinter fish and hardy plants in cold climates.

6. Marginal shelf Partial shelf 12 inches deep; for plants that thrive in shallow water.

Streams in the Landscape

A stream or brook, as it carries water attractively from one place to another, creates a delightful combination of sight and sound that brings life to the landscape. As water trickles over stones, sometimes beginning at a waterfall and ending in a pond, it may be slow and calming or rushing and energizing. The sound of even the smallest stream will draw people toward it, even if it's not in clear sight.

A formal stream, such as a straight channel lined with cut stone, might course through a patio or edge a terrace. Whether it ends in a decorative pool with a fountain or not, it creates a serene atmosphere. The shallow water in a stream also attracts birds and other wildlife.

A rocky streambed is often most interesting if it is not visible all at once. When it meanders across the land, flowing around a tree here and dropping over a slope there, it looks more natural. A stream works especially well where there's a slight slope to the terrain that brings the power of gravity to the water feature, coaxing its flow and fall.

This stream design helps meld the hardscape patio with its surroundings. If you plan to build a stone patio, consider including a formal rill that follows a meandering path across the area.

Waterfalls add music and speed to a stream's movement. A series of petite falls sends this stream zipping through the landscape.

When making a stream, rock-lined curves and bends create a natural appearance. As water flows over the stones, delightful sounds rise from the movement.

The type of moving water suitable for a particular landscape depends on the scale and layout of the setting. Large landscapes can hold streams and waterfalls of great size. A smaller urban or suburban garden would be better suited to a small but mesmerizing trickle.

Any stream or waterfall adds a strong design element that should be integrated with the size, style, and materials of the setting. Use rocks to help incorporate the stream into the landscape. Place them in groups here and there along the edge to hold and conceal the liner and give you a platform where you can perform maintenance. Situate large flat stones, firmly installed, to form a path across the stream. Larger stones in the stream direct and channel water; smaller stones create ripples. For more details about creating a waterfall, see pages 168–171.

Placing rocks on the outside of a stream's curve creates more turbulence there. Rocks may also be used to decrease the width of a stream, making the water flow faster.

The narrowness of the side yard precluded both a walkway and a stream. As a result, broad stepping-stones provide firm footing to traverse the space.

Use Rocks and Boulders to Direct a Stream

The basic components of a stream—its underlayment, liner, pump, and pipe—and the natural elements of rocks and plants work together to make a realistic watercourse. The stream's source might be a waterfall, pond, or bog. Or the water could appear to emerge from a bed of rock that actually disguises the stream's pump housing. Connected via a direct-as-possible pipeline to the bottom of the watercourse, the pump recirculates water to the stream head (top). A catch basin, whether below ground or above, should be large enough to hold all the stream's water when the pump is shut off.

Although rocks placed in the stream can trap debris, forming a dam and forcing water over the bank, they also contribute to a natural-looking design. Make the stream wider at curves, narrower at a straight run for a natural look. Avoid long stretches of shallow water where algae will build up if the current is too leisurely.

The placement of boulders and a range of various-size rocks should appear random. Let small stones and gravel fill in between medium and large rocks. The size of rocks you select to make a waterfall will affect its sound (see page 171 for details).

Adding a mix of foliage and flowering plantings alongside a newly installed streambed makes it look instantly established. Spaces between stones form planting pockets for a wide assortment of plants, including perennials and bulbs. Large shrubs may eventually arch over the water, as they would in the wild.

CONSERVATION STRATEGIES FOR WATER FEATURES

Water in a stream, pond, or other feature evaporates and must be replenished periodically. To minimize evaporation, choose a site in partial shade and incorporate a drainage casement or dry well (a pit lined with gravel) to catch any overflow. Think twice about including a fountain that sprays water into the air as the spray feature will cause the water to quickly evaporate. Look for areas where a stream or pond could overflow after a heavy rain or a power failure that stops the pump. Containing the stream is vital to avoid waste and to reduce the frequency of replenishing the water.

This stream helps funnel water from a hillside well to an adjoining pond. To avoid problems from excess water, it's usually best to avoid locating a water feature at the base of a slope.

Build a Dry Stream

A dry streambed, which mimics the real thing but has water in it only after a heavy rain, is a practical alternative constructed in much the same way as a water-filled stream. A dry stream suggests water movement without the actual flow, pump, or piping.

A dry creek bed can border the perimeter of your yard or flow across a portion of it without emptying into a pond. The most natural-looking dry creek will have a meandering path, irregular edges, and varying width. Laying heavy-duty landscape fabric over the 6- to 8-inch-deep excavation will help deter weeds. Top the landscape fabric with a 1-inch layer of pea gravel. If you prefer to have a usually dry stream that is made to channel storm water into a garden and support plant life along its edges, spread underlayment and a flexible liner over the site. Top the liner with a 1-inch layer of pea gravel.

If your landscape is flat, consider developing the terrain to create a slope, if only a slight one where the stream will run. Place boulders randomly and then group various-size stones around them. Use the boulders to help hold the edges of the stream's liner in place. Fill in with gravel. Use rough stone to achieve the look of a long-dry creek; rounded, tumbled, smooth stones will enhance the illusion of an active stream. Soften the edges of the stream with groundcovers and perennials that will spread without rooting in the stream.

This formerly muddy-when-wet narrow side yard was transformed with a streambed that helps channel rainwater runoff into planted areas.

Meandering through the entryway sidewalk, this dry stream is both functional and eye-pleasing. The stream is lined with tumbled river rock and nestled between flagstone pavers.

A strategically placed slab enables visitors to ford this streambed, whether it holds water or not. The bridge adds to the feature's picturesque quality and functionality by making it simple to cross.

BUILD A DRY STREAM

You don't need water to enjoy a meandering stream. A dry stream has a similar beauty and is a great feature for highlighting favorite stones and boulders. The stream illustrated below is designed to be dry. Create a dry stream for carrying away storm water by replacing the landscape fabric with underlayment and a flexible liner.

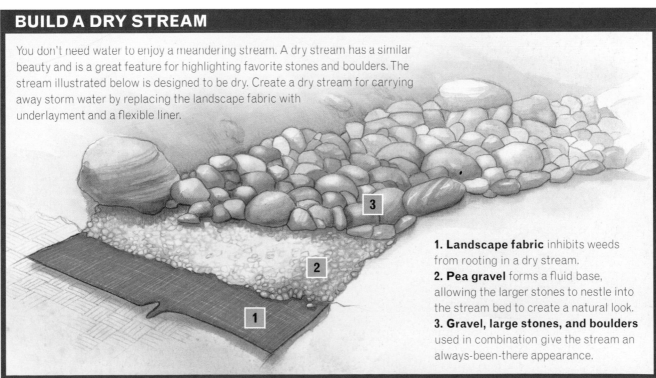

1. Landscape fabric inhibits weeds from rooting in a dry stream.

2. Pea gravel forms a fluid base, allowing the larger stones to nestle into the stream bed to create a natural look.

3. Gravel, large stones, and boulders used in combination give the stream an always-been-there appearance.

Multiple waterfalls add captivating and exciting elements to the landscape with their movement and sound give this swimming pool a natural look.

Waterfalls in the Landscape

The most dramatic feature involving stone and water is a waterfall. Water flowing over a drop in level creates soothing sounds and adds intriguing movement to a setting. Stones provide the exit points for water as it leaves one level and falls to the next. The dramatic qualities of a waterfall depend on the height and slope of the stone the water tumbles over.

Waterfalls come in many styles, shapes, and sizes. Falls look most natural when built on a slope, flowing from one level to another, whether in a low, gentle tumble or a steep, cascading rush. Take advantage of a slope by designing a stream with a series of waterfalls ending in a pond. The simplest, single-step waterfall typically flows into a pond that serves as a reservoir for it, but you can make a pondless waterfall as well. In this case, the water is pumped from a buried reservoir at the bottom to the top of the waterfall. Your falls may flow between two ponds or as a single spillway surrounded by an outcropping or a rock garden. Where there are rough rocks and tumbling water, a natural effect can be achieved even without a steep slope. If your property is level, consider excavating for a pond and saving the soil to sculpt berms and other raised terrain for a watercourse that appears to have been shaped by nature.

If your landscape leans toward the more formal side of design, you might prefer geometric elements. Options include a straight-sided channel, stair-stepped falls, or a wall with water sliding over it. The cut stone that suits formal features mixes well with metal, tile, acrylic, glass, or recycled materials.

This stacked-stone wall, complete with falling rivulets, frames a formal backdrop for a stone patio in a wooded setting.

Make Music with a Waterfall

The lip of a waterfall, called a spill stone, is the main stone that the water pours over. The spill stone determines the characteristics of the waterfall. If it is a flat rock with a smooth, slick edge, water moves over the spill stone in a sheet with no interruptions. If the spill stone is jagged and sharp, water flows over it in divided streamlets. Water will flow down the face of rounded rock.

Most waterfalls are part of other water features, such as streams and ponds. The type of rocks you select for your waterfall should match those used to make the rest of the feature. Also choose rocks that are in scale with the setting. The size and shape of each rock affect the way water falls over it and the sound of the falling water.

Limit your waterfall's height to 1 to 2 feet to keep it natural looking and to limit water loss as it splashes. It's possible to plan for five or six falls over several yards. Falls higher than 3 feet should be reserved for large ponds with extremely powerful pumps. When your plans for a water feature include a waterfall, make sure the recirculating pump has adequate capacity to move the volume of water uphill. The waterfall will also need to be lined with a flexible pond liner to prevent leakage.

Depending on the design of a water feature, waterfalls are constructed as part of the watercourse, which may be a tiered stream or may consist of a series of small pools linked by cascades. As water recirculates, it is pumped from the lowest point via tubing to the highest point.

The multiple waterfalls in this stream send water rushing toward a small pond. The waterfalls play an important role in the feature's water filtration—the movement helps remove debris and increases oxygenation (discouraging algae growth).

WATER MUSIC

You can alter the sound of a waterfall by notching or changing the shape of the spill stone and by placing stones at the base, where the water hits.

Alter the water's volume by making the catch basin or pond deeper or shallower, sloping the watercourse as it flows into the basin or adjusting the flow of water.

To form an echo chamber that amplifies the falling water's sound, cantilever a flat spill stone several inches over the edge of the pond 6 inches or more above the water. Tuck another flat stone against the side of the pond to form the vertical back of the chamber. Stack rocks about 2 inches high on the cantilevered stone, tilting them slightly toward the water.

Other options include a fountain situated in or on a wall or centered in a formal shallow pool. A self-contained fountain in a watertight bowl or pot is the easiest to make. If you add a fountain to a pond or a watercourse, it will aerate the water, preventing it from becoming stagnant.

The water feature, built to resemble a natural grotto, follows the incline of the site. The waterfall pours down a rock ledge, then spills over the boulders and into the pond.

A stream harnesses the power of gravity by flowing a modest slope, tumbling over falls, and trickling through turns before being pumped back to its point of origin.

Fountains in the Landscape

One of the easiest ways to get your feet wet combining stone and water in the landscape is to add a fountain to a pond or garden bed. The splashing sound and subtle movement of water bring another dimension to a garden that's enjoyable with or without a pond. A recirculating pump accomplishes seemingly magical feats with water. Fountain heads produce a variety of spray patterns, from a fine spray to a slow bubbling to a gushing plume of water.

Above all, place a fountain where its sight, sound, and motion will be most appreciated. A fountain instantly changes the atmosphere by masking nearby street noise and inducing serenity. Since fountains have become increasingly popular, it's easy to find a wide range of ready-made styles.

You'll find fountains of all sizes and styles. If you select a fountain that has strong sculptural qualities, such as a stone urn or statuary, it will be attractive even when the water isn't flowing. A stone basin or boulder fountain, with water bubbling over it and into a reservoir hidden underneath, is ideal for an entryway, patio, courtyard, or a secluded garden room. A tabletop or upright fountain would be perfect for a deck.

Drilled and stacked flagstones form a charmingly simple fountain. The water spills over the stones and into an underground reservoir.

A veritable homage to stone—collected from the site as well as on travels—stands as a rocky sculpture in the landscape. Turning it into a cascading fountain gives the creation a wet and wild character.

BUILD A BOULDER FOUNTAIN

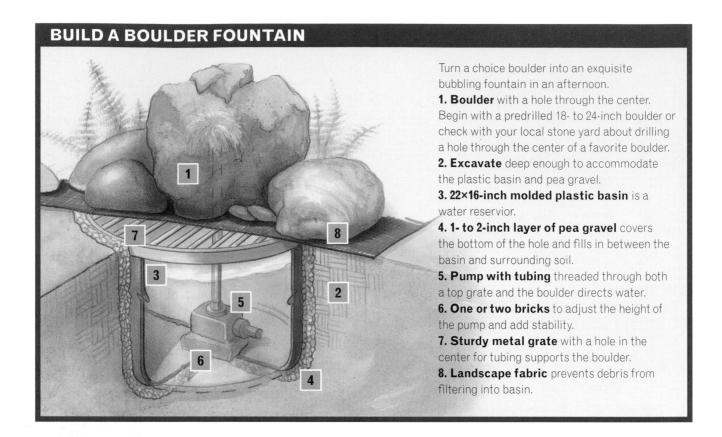

Turn a choice boulder into an exquisite bubbling fountain in an afternoon.

1. Boulder with a hole through the center. Begin with a predrilled 18- to 24-inch boulder or check with your local stone yard about drilling a hole through the center of a favorite boulder.

2. Excavate deep enough to accommodate the plastic basin and pea gravel.

3. 22×16-inch molded plastic basin is a water reservoir.

4. 1- to 2-inch layer of pea gravel covers the bottom of the hole and fills in between the basin and surrounding soil.

5. Pump with tubing threaded through both a top grate and the boulder directs water.

6. One or two bricks to adjust the height of the pump and add stability.

7. Sturdy metal grate with a hole in the center for tubing supports the boulder.

8. Landscape fabric prevents debris from filtering into basin.

This boulder fountain sits at the headwater of a pebble stream that flows through a bluestone sidewalk. A hole drilled through the center of the boulder and pipe directs water up through the boulder and over the surface.

Add a Fountain to Your Garden

Whatever type of fountain you choose, you'll need three pieces of equipment: the right size pump to handle the volume of water in the pond or other reservoir, the fountain tubing to connect the pump to the fountain, and an electrical outlet that includes a ground fault circuit interrupter (GFCI), unless your fountain is solar powered.

If you opt for a fountain made with large garden statuary, it must be set on a solid base of concrete or stone for stability and plumbed accordingly. Any fountain should be positioned so that its spray falls within the confines of the pool or reservoir beneath it for water conservation. Shelter the fountain from wind to help prevent the water from blowing away and emptying the pool on windy days. If the water sprays onto a nearby walkway, it could become slippery and create a hazard. Locate the fountain and pump where you can reach them easily for maintenance. The water in your fountain should be topped off periodically.

In regions where winter brings freezing temperatures, the fountain must be drained and protected from freeze-thaw cycles. This may entail storing the pump indoors.

Water in a tsukubai, a traditional Japanese fountain featuring a bamboo spout and crouching basin, trickles into the stout container and overflows into a reservoir hidden below it.

A formerly flat backyard now features a stream, waterfalls, and two ponds encircled by stone pathways. Eighty tons of rock make up the terrain and give the water features greater dimension.

Landscape Visit: Water Wonder

It took 10 minutes and a can of paint to come up with a bold concept for transforming a backyard in Edmonds, Washington. A rough sketch and a sense of adventure were transferred to an outline on the grass for two ponds and a creek—the beginnings of a complete makeover. Five seasons and 80 tons of rock later, the backyard is anything but boring.

A crew of landscape professionals used a backhoe to excavate the yard, carving out the two ponds and a connecting stream roughly 24 feet long. The excavated soil was shaped into several "hills;" the tallest supports a 3-foot-high waterfall, positioned for viewing from the deck at the back of the house.

Carefully situated benches like this invite visitors to take in the vistas along the streams and ponds. At the back of the house a boxwood hedge skirts the deck and affords privacy.

Landscape Visit (continued)

Once the crane wrestled the largest of the boulders into place, a worker lined the ponds and stream with gunite (a blend of sand and portland cement that's denser and more waterproof than standard concrete). The homeowner spent the winter installing electrical lines and an irrigation system. Then the new layout was topped with loose rock of all sizes for a natural effect.

Over the next year, plantings were added gradually. Large evergreens, Japanese maples, and flowering shrubs finished the basic structure of the garden. Remaining spaces were filled in with perennials and bulbs. Now all the elements work together as an ideal landscape that begs to be explored and discovered. A path leads around a bend to a narrow trail and eventually a bench—a destination with lovely views. From there, the sound of a waterfall beckons—to the next bench and the next vista.

The flagstone path intersects with a cascading stream and steps its way around the backyard. Blue star creeper and Corsican mint fill in between the stones.

A narrow path along the side of the stream leads to a vantage point that reveals the lower pond. Across the pond, color contrasts in stones and plants adds interest to the setting.

Small surprises, such as a cherubic statue tucked in a corner of the stream, bring delight to visitors.

7

Rock and

It's easy to find a home for stone in most gardens. Making a garden among stones—from grainy gravel to artful boulders—presents one of the most promising opportunities to combine plants with rock just as nature might. You'll likely appreciate the natural beauty that comes with this ancient pairing of aesthetic opposites—hard and soft, neutral and colorful, inert and lively.

Beyond appearances, you'll also like the way that rocks create nurturing microclimates for plants, enabling you to grow plants that would ordinarily be challenged to survive. What's more, a rock garden gives you a beautiful way to cope with harsh conditions or a problematic slope. In the end, rock and gravel gardens are often comparatively low-maintenance landscapes.

Gravel Gardens

Gardening with Rock

Rock gardens are not one style but several, including classic alpine, Asian, those on naturally rocky sites (slopes, slabs, and scree), and gravel. Each yields a different effect, but all share natural elements and an overall natural look. And all have time-tested, historic antecedents that continue to inspire beautiful, practical designs for all or part of a landscape.

Traditional rock gardens resemble mountainside growing conditions with sturdy alpine plants sprouting from pockets of soil between rocks ranging from pebbles to small boulders. Accustomed to challenging conditions, these compact plants typically require little fertilizer or supplemental water. The textural tapestry of the typical mat-forming or shrubby plants with subtle coloring blends marvelously with rock in nearly any setting. Beds mulched with gravel preserve soil moisture and suppress weeds, demanding less maintenance than average.

A range of Asian-derived garden styles—especially those of China and Japan—present intriguing options, from a spare area of raked gravel to a sprawling landscape covered with rough boulders. Centered on the use of stone as a building material with aesthetic and symbolic value, an Asian-style garden offers opportunities for spiritual growth as well as planting.

Planting among rocks on a slope, in between slabs, or in scree and gravel creates the most natural-looking of all rocky gardens. If you are drawn to such wild places as rugged coastlines, deserts, and mountains, let nature inspire you: Take advantage of the ideal well-draining conditions of these rubble-rich landscaping possibilities.

Stones and boulders hold a sunbaked slope and create natural pockets of warmth for cactus, alpines, and dwarf conifers to dig into with their shallow roots.

Layered into the crevices here, plants include madwort, sea pink, *Acantholimon venustum*, and dwarf shore pine. Bedrock forms the beginning of a splendid landscape when you think of it as an asset (rather than a problem) and use it as the basis of an alpine garden.

Boulders mark the way, bringing a sense of strength and welcome to those who pass by. An entry garden establishes the front yard as a transition from hectic world to tranquil sanctuary.

A gravel garden accented with wall stone and angular boulders accommodates a collection of cactus. Soft conifers serve as a backdrop for the rockscape.

Make an Easy-Care Garden with Gravel

A gravel garden typically features gravel combined with a few large stones and plants. Depending on the grade of gravel, it may be raked into a pattern in the tradition of a Zen garden. A gravel garden may be an open expanse—a floor of pebbles—much like a path or patio, accented by carefully placed islands of rock and select plants. Or it could be a small, tranquil setting such as a courtyard or side yard designed for contemplation. A nearby bench, deck, or window provides a viewing station. If you live in a coastal region—or wish you did—a beachy garden, complete with fine gravel, driftwood, and ornamental grasses, may fulfill your dream of a landscape. As an alternative, consider a landscape design with graphic flair. It's easily accomplished by laying out patterns using different colors, sizes, and shapes of gravel and keeping them separate with edging.

Ideal for warm climates such as desert, high-desert, or Mediterranean, a gravel garden proves adaptable wherever hot, dry weather prevails at least part of the year. A gravel garden also shines during wet periods when the stone's finer qualities are revealed and the bed drains readily.

For a raked design, select fine (⅛- to ½-inch) gravel or finer poultry grit. Otherwise, opt for pea gravel, larger river rock, or a combination of these washed materials. Add boulders in groups of two or three as accents. Widely spaced stepping-stones prove practical.

When it comes to plants, sprinkle them here and there, relating them to the boulders for best effect. Plant dwarf evergreens for year-round color, spring-flowering trees and bulbs for transient color, and drought-tolerant dwarf perennials for longer-lasting summer and fall displays.

Although gravel behaves like mulch by preserving soil moisture and deterring weeds, periodic maintenance—including raking and weeding—is necessary.

Dwarf conifers and native plants thrive alongside winter-hardy cactus in this gravel garden. Winter-hardy cacti grow in a sunny spot with good soil.

Explore East Asian-Style Rock Gardens

The East Asian way of rock gardening, based on centuries of tradition and practice, is a homage to nature. The style and aesthetics of the gardens have been influenced by philosophy, religion, and ritual ways of life in China and Japan over generations. East Asian-style continues to evolve not as a single form but as a spiritual approach that takes form in natural elements.

There are various types of East Asian rock gardens, from strolling grounds to miniature landscapes in containers. All are carefully arranged. Some Japanese Zen designs, known as dry or gravel gardens, are composed entirely of stone, including a mix of sand, gravel, and more substantial rock. The finer materials are used for dramatic contrast and beauty—raked gravel represents flowing water. Thoughtfully chosen larger rocks, honored symbols of mountains or islands, are deliberately placed to make a statement and delight the senses.

The natural look of East Asian rock gardens is only part of the picture. The feel of the setting—serene, graceful, harmonious—is another aspect that appeals often to Westerners and inspires them to re-create it. You may seek to study and practice Eastern traditions in gardening or merely adapt the style and aesthetics into your landscape. Whether you want to dedicate a portion of your yard to a Japanese garden or guide your overall landscape design through Asian influences, keep it simple.

Simplicity guides this Asian garden design. The green and brown color scheme highlights the pebbles and boulders that form the paths and artistic elements.

Massed plantings, including juniper and woolly thyme, lay the simple groundwork for an Asian-influenced garden, in which a single focus stone and a pebble path stand out.

JOY OF RAKING

Over the centuries Zen practitioners have discovered the joy of creating rockscapes as a practice of mindfulness and meditation. A serene state comes from raking gravel smooth and then scratching gentle curves, even straights, and endless circles. The act of raking over and over leads one to a meditative center of peace.

Raked gravel gardens take a less-is-more approach to artful landscaping. A wide-tooth wooden rake is used to make wavelike patterns in the fine gravel.

East Asian-Style Rock Gardens (continued)

The solid, anchored look of East Asian gardens is achieved in large part by using stone as the primary building material. A combination of gravel and stone, while simple, requires careful design. As you begin to plan, ask yourself: Will the garden allow you to walk on it or merely sit nearby and view it? Will it include a stream composed of gravel or water? Are you aiming for a traditional, minimalist Zen garden, or do you seek to balance clean, simple lines of boulders and small trees and shrubs with your home's architecture? How would a stone path, bridge, or wall fit into the scheme?

Once you have considered your goals and the parameters of the site, determine the size and components of your rock garden. Whether it will involve the entire landscape or a small corner of it, allow the Eastern less-is-more philosophy to guide your choices. Remember, you can make an effective garden using only rock and gravel. Use a minimum of materials and aim for unity to get the desired effect. Add plants and ornaments as trimmings. Include a water feature, such as a stone basin or a boulder fountain, to enhance a serene atmosphere.

Select stones for their silhouettes as well as their color and texture. For a dry creek or path, choose large (1- to 1½-inch) gravel. Lay patterns of smooth beach stones for contrast. Group boulders in twos and threes to create large focal points. Place these treasured rocks vertically or horizontally, depending on each one's size, shape, and unique characteristics.

PLANTS FOR AN EAST ASIAN-STYLE ROCK GARDEN

1. Azalea (*Rhododendron* spp.)
Dwarf shrub varieties with rounded forms thrive in well-drained acid soil and part sun. Prolific blooms in spring; colors vary depending on variety. Zones 3–10.

2. Crocus (*Crocus* spp.)
Spring- and fall-flowering bulbs that produce grassy foliage and typically purple, yellow, or white egg-shape blooms on 3- to 4-inch stems; in full sun to part shade. Zones 3–8.

3. Juniper (*Juniperus* spp.)
Low, spreading varieties with rich green or gray-green needles. Tough evergreens tolerant of most conditions. Zones 2–10, depending on variety.

4. Maiden grass (*Miscanthus sinensis* 'Gracillimus')
Ornamental grass that forms tall, narrow, or fountain-shape clumps with sometimes silvery leaves; pinkish plumes in fall. Varieties from 3 to 6 feet tall. Zones 5–9.

5. Pine (*Pinus* spp.)
Dwarf *P. mugo* has a rounded, tufted appearance; *P. banksiana* is a small, weeping tree. Best in full sun. Zones 2–10, depending on variety.

6. Siberian iris (*Iris sibirica*)
A 2×2-foot perennial with grasslike leaves and late-spring, early-summer blooms. In full sun to shade; tolerates most soil but thrives in moist conditions. Zones 3–9.

Within a wooden privacy fence, a quiet, relaxing garden distinguished by Japanese flair covers a small suburban lot. The stone-studded oasis includes a trickling stream.

Gravel, sand, and fieldstones combine with texture-rich plants in this Japanese Zen garden. The simple green plants highlight the unique characteristics of the stones.

A rock-strewn oceanside slope sustains a classic alpine garden. This rugged hillside terrain is passable by a series of stone steps.

Create a Rock Garden for Your Climate

Picture a landscape covered with gravel and various-size stones—some rugged boulders—and diminutive flowering plants cropping up among the rock. This is a rock garden. Adaptable to most climates, this nature-inspired form of gardening plays the dramatic contrasts between ancient and ephemeral; hard and soft. Influenced by distinctive plants in mountain settings, early rock gardeners attempted to replicate alpine scenes. Rock gardening today extends beyond alpine plants and focuses on creating a special habitat for plants that thrive in rocky conditions and your region's climate.

Your rock garden may include small perennial beds enhanced with fieldstones and large gravel. A rock garden can solve landscape issues. Sloping ground and hot, dry, windblown sites that ordinarily present challenges are ideal for rock gardens.

Alpine plants are the traditional heart of a rock garden. But you can establish a beautiful, easy-care garden with a few showy, reliable perennials, grasses, and shrubs—adding bulbs and annuals for seasonal color. Rock gardening requires patience—it takes time for plants to become established and fill in among the rocks because many alpine varieties are slow growing.

Aided by compost-enriched soil, a tapestry of dwarf phlox, dianthus, heather, and other alpines withstands constant wind and salt spray that batter this hillside garden.

Make Good Drainage a Priority

The conditions that usually create challenges for gardeners are ideal for a rock garden: lots of sun and wind, a slope, and extreme drainage. Good drainage is key when growing alpines, many herbs, and other plants that tend to flourish in a rock garden. Before you add rocks when making your rock garden, amend the soil with loads of peat, shredded leaves, sand, grit, crushed rock, or pumice so it will drain very well.

Otherwise, you don't need special conditions in order to create a rock garden. You'll need gravel and rock, of course, but beyond that, you can build a garden to suit your site, the climate, and the type of plants you want to grow. You might make your rock garden with native perennials or diminutive varieties of them. Dwarf and prostrate shrubs, especially evergreens, some heaths and heathers, and cinquefoil, mountain laurel, and cotoneaster, contribute incomparable character.

Mulch around plants with gravel to minimize water loss, reduce frost heave, improve drainage, and set the stage for more rock. Add clumps of rocks to form natural-looking arrangements. Bury the largest rocks to the widest part of their girth for best effect.

A rock and gravel garden flourishes where plant roots can reach soil pockets between the stones.

SIX GREAT ALPINE PLANTS FOR ROCK GARDENS

Tough and drought-tolerant, most alpine plants come from places with extreme climates. They'll withstand intense sunlight, thin soil, frigid winters, and drying winds.

1. Bellflower (*Campanula* spp.) Four inches tall with a profusion of blue-purple bell-shape flowers in early summer. Zones 4–8.

2. Candytuft (*Iberis sempervirens*) This low-growing evergreen features white flowers in spring. Shear after blooming to encourage a repeat show in fall. Zones 4–9.

3. Lewisia (*Lewisia* spp.) Evergreen or deciduous leaves, depending on the species. Funnel-shaped white, pink, yellow, or orange flowers in spring. Zones 4–8, depending on species.

4. Maiden pink (*Dianthus deltoides*) Grassy, low-growing green leaves that spread and give rise to hot pink flowers from late spring through early summer. Zones 4–9.

5. Stonecrop (*Sedum* spp.) Spreading from a crown of succulent leaves, ground-hugging varieties drape over rocks and walls. Some fleshy leaves tinged burgundy; flowers pink or yellow. Many cultivars of this easy-to-grow plant. Zones 4–9.

6. Rock speedwell (*Veronica fruticans*) This mat-forming perennial is 3 to 6 inches tall and spreads to 2 feet or more; features dainty blue flowers in summer. Zones 4–9.

Winter-hardy cactus and the cheerful, bright-hued lewisia blossoms add color and texture to this rock-filled landscape. Lewisia blooms with gusto in spring and then retreats underground in the heat of summer.

Ideas for Slopes, Slabs, and Scree

Any of three popular features can be incorporated into a larger rock garden or serve as a complete rock garden by itself. A slope, slab, or scree should be in proportion to the whole landscape. In most cases, start by thinking larger rather than smaller. Keep in mind that mature plants, especially full-size trees and shrubs, make smaller stones appear less prominent. The effect is minimized when using dwarf plant varieties.

A slope, or rock garden set into a natural incline, can be installed on a hill or berm of any size. It resembles a natural outcropping with several boulders or masses of stone. A slope functions like a retaining wall but works more attractively to hold a hill and control erosion. For best effect, use one type of stone, varying the sizes. If striated, set each stone so the lines run in the same direction, parallel to the ground, for a natural look.

A slab is an all-stone feature comprising pieces arranged to resemble a large, single outcropping that has split over time. Depending on the size, slabs should be placed where they will be noticed, whether to appear subtle or powerful. They look natural set on a flat expanse or a slope. Less dense stone, such as limestone, can be split along natural fractures into multiple slabs. Plant the gaps between the stones with low-growing varieties.

A scree is a prominent outcropping that resembles piles of stone sometimes found at the base of a cliff or bluff and includes few, if any, plants. Crushed gravel mulches the ground around the boulders and smaller rocks. A scree looks most natural at the base of a long slope and can be constructed on a gentle slope. Plant the top portion of the slope with evergreen trees and shrubs to create a rugged, mountainous appearance.

Small stones planted among shrubs and groundcovers help stabilize this front yard slope. Various sizes of stones can be integrated into a slope and will stay in place if they are partially buried.

Small boulders and low-maintenance perennials appear to tumble playfully down this steep slope. The stones and plants serve an important purpose. They prevent erosion by holding the soil in place.

Slabs of stone and gravel fill the space between this fence and the sidewalk. Attractive stone slabs turn tough-to-landscape areas, like this narrow strip of land, into easy-care spaces.

A small wooden portal, called a humbling gate because people must bow to pass through it, frames a glimpse into the Zen-style courtyard garden beyond.

Landscape Visit: Zen Inspiration

Careful selection of key elements twined the walled entryway of a new home into a restful refuge. Her heart set on a simple Zen-inspired garden, the homeowner found a landscape designer who helped marry the disparate styles of an Italianate-villa-style house on the Northern California coast to a Japanese-style landscape.

Characterized by natural beauty and artful vignettes, the secluded garden room has become a source of peaceful relaxation. The homeowners enjoy the garden as a place for practicing meditation and yoga, taking leisurely strolls with their children, and also entertaining friends. Their personal sanctuary includes treasures from world travels. An aged stone Buddha exudes an air of tranquillity. Pieces of wall art, a prayer bell, and Japanese stone lanterns accent the garden.

A stone-slab bridge links the two sides of this garden bisected by a dry creek. A burgundy Japanese maple and russet Japanese blood grass are among the plants repeated throughout the landscape for continuity.

Landscape Visit (continued)

In the tradition of Japanese Zen-style gardening, a complete and unified landscape fills a small space with illusions of grandeur and time-weathered character. This is accomplished largely by using stone for various purposes throughout the setting. Large stepping-stones form meandering pathways. Boulders peek and rise from the moss-covered terrain. Tumbled pebbles create a symbolic stream. A massive stone slab bridges the stream and provides an organic yoga mat.

The palette of plants, repeated throughout the garden, helps simplify and unify the landscape design. A carpet of moss, creeping thyme, and prostrate evergreens meld earth, stones, and other plantings into a soft, harmonious setting.

The blue-green and blue-gray stones lining this dry stream mimic water with their smooth, flowing appearance.

Japanese-style gardens derive part of their symbolic meaning from ornaments such as the stone Buddha at the back of this courtyard.

A stone bench offers a place to sit and meditate. The courtyard wall provides a backrest. A nearby ponytail asparagus fern is one of the plants repeated throughout the landscape as a unifying element.

8

Boulders and

It's no wonder that big stones have been raised to sacred stature since ancient times—their majesty is powerful. Stone accents, including large rocks and massive boulders as well as cast, carved, and naturally wrought stone accents, add beauty to a landscape in exchange for no watering, weeding, or other maintenance.

The color, shape, and surface texture of a stone accent works with plants to create a harmonious expression with lasting value. When you take advantage of stones' artful qualities, huge slabs can form earthy garden furniture and vertical statuary can raise the drama factor. As prominent features, your artful accents may also be given more earthly tasks: marking an entry, bolstering security, preventing erosion, and attracting wildlife, among others.

Stone Accents

Boulders and Accents in the Landscape

The versatility of stone enables you to incorporate it as a feature with tremendous ornamental and practical value. One massive stone may represent a mountain or island in the midst of an Asian-style garden, while a pair of boulders flanking an entryway makes a strong welcoming statement just about anywhere. When serving as a focal point, a boulder that sits at the end of the driveway works as an address landmark; a slab sprawling alongside a path as edging provides a place to sit and rest.

Boulders have sculptural qualities benefiting their use alone or in groups. A carved stone basin holds enough water to attract birds as a place to drink and bathe. A few outstanding stones can be arranged in an artistic display or one that resembles a natural outcropping. Standing on end, upright stones also work as retainers, but many are called into more sculptural service. A composition's degree of naturalness depends largely on the way plants are used to marry the stone and the site (see page 206, "Planting Around Boulders").

Sometimes boulders have inherent qualities that set them apart. One might have a recess deep enough to hold water or a plant. Its shape might suggest a giant fish or a human face. Boulders can be cut or carved into bowls, lanterns, faces, and other forms—recognizable or abstract—that add a sense of intrigue, surprise, human-imbued whimsy, or antiquity to a garden. You might purchase an impressive piece of statuary or thoughtfully stack stones to form classic cairns or "ancient" ruins. As one-of-a-kind garden art, stone accents a landscape with lasting appeal.

Individually placed boulders edge the aggregate steps of this dramatic Japanese-influenced entryway.

A trio of stones, each of a different size and shape, clusters around a small Japanese maple. The grouping would also work effectively without the tree at its center if the stones were placed closer to each other.

Planting pockets between massive granite boulders are home to a host of colorful perennials. These boulders are part of the natural landscape. Soil was added to the cracks and crevices to allow plants to grow.

Landscape Design Ideas for Boulders

Usually defined by their size and shape, boulders are typically 100- to 3,000-pound stones. The size and shape of boulders affect their potential use in the landscape and their contribution to a composition. A rounded, chunky mound integrates well with areas of gravel, garden, or water. Low, flat, horizontal stones make peaceful islands that may function as seating or pedestals for another garden accent. Other shapes include irregular or arching stones that suggest movement and work well as dramatic elements next to steps or a water feature. Vertical stones bring strength and excitement to a setting with their height.

Rather than plop a single boulder at a front corner of your yard to discourage people from cutting across the lawn and wearing a path, consider making that rock a star elsewhere in the landscape. Group it with two other smaller-yet-similar boulders to form a stellar trio that will appear more like a natural outcropping than an oddity. Keep in mind that it is simplest to install outcroppings before putting in plants.

Look beyond large stones' aesthetic qualities for their functional applications. Boulders—large or small—help define the edge of steps or a paved area. The strength of boulders makes them ideal wall-building material, whether massed or carefully stacked. Massive chunks of stone placed along a property line, driveway, or parking area form a secure barrier. Grouped along the edge of a pond or the course of a stream, boulders create the sense of scale and perspective found in nature.

Massive boulders skirt a limestone patio and wall, creating a unique stone privacy screen.

Placed side by side, boulders form an informal retaining wall. Drought-tolerant lantana, Mexican bush sage, daylily, Dahlberg daisy, and sedum thrive in the planting pockets between the boulders.

Boulders appear to grow alongside perennials and small trees in this garden. The boulders are partially buried for a natural look.

Although these boulders appear to have tumbled into place, they were carefully positioned. Successfully placing a large rock requires planting it to its widest point and orienting it to maximize its shape in the landscape.

Curbside gardens and shapely boulders transform this formerly barren swath of land along the street into a lush oasis.

PLANTING AROUND BOULDERS

One of the surest ways to make a stone appear as if Mother Nature placed it is to plant its edges. Trees and shrubs provide instant anchors and eventual frames. Ornamental grasses and perennials offset and balance stones' spacing. Groundcovers—including landscape roses and low-growing evergreens—soften and finish a display.

A simple combination of these types of plants will complement an outcropping. Just as you wouldn't want to dump a pile of stones at the edge of a planting area or line a bed with a string of stone, the same holds true for plants. Integrate plantings among rocks rather than ringing them with same-size plants.

Plants benefit when placed in the pockets between boulders, where moisture collects. Sometimes rocks create a microclimate for plants, providing the extra warmth and protection they need to thrive.

Plant Boulders in the Landscape

Boulders add interest and vitality to a landscape, whether you choose to highlight their individual character, display a select group, or mass them for maximum impact. Whatever your goal, if you want the effect of the stone to appear as natural as possible, use the following guidelines to help accomplish this.

Take a nature walk to gather inspiration. Notice how boulders festoon a creek bed, shouldering one another, or slant in hulking masses along the bank. Typically, one-third to two-thirds of a boulder hides below ground. Follow this lead by burying a broad or chunky stone up to its widest point to create the most natural effect and lasting stability. When standing a vertical stone dramatically on end, plant it in a pocket of compacted subsoil backfilled with gravel and rubble. Then mound soil at its base to complete the planting. Some stone, such as limestone, has natural striations that guide you to placing it with the lines parallel to the ground.

Grouping boulders in odd numbers—three, five, seven, nine—works best. Place the same kind of stones together because pieces of granite or limestone, for instance, would most likely be found together in nature. Vary the sizes and shapes of stones in a group. A classic combination includes a large upright, a middle-size mound, and a small horizontal. Grounded in a complementing base of gravel or mounded earth, the arrangement needs only the finishing touch of plants.

Boulders line the far edge of this swimming pool, creating a pleasing transition from the manicured lawn to the woodland beyond. Boulders also form a waterfall at one end of the pool.

Find the Perfect Boulder

Most people don't have a natural trove of boulders sitting around on their property. If you're fortunate enough to unearth a cache of stones in the process of excavating for a new home, have the builder set the boulders aside or arrange them on the site for you. By the same token, if natural outcroppings of bedrock already bring character to your landscape, take advantage of the potential for well-draining conditions. Allow the bedrock to shape planting beds, and add soil on top of it.

Otherwise, when selecting boulders for your landscape, look for unusual specimens with interesting shapes, crevices, or textures. Craggy, weathered stones with a patina of moss or lichen bring instant age to a new landscape. Avoid stones that crumble at the edges when handling—especially those containing mica—they won't weather well. If your landscape design calls for more than one stone, look for boulders that complement each other—consider size, shape, and color.

Stone suppliers often set aside especially colorful, striped, or naturally weathered boulders to sell as accents. Study these specimens from all possible angles and imagine how you could place them in your landscape to show their best aspects or otherwise put them to work. The cost of stone for accent pieces varies greatly, depending on its size and type, but it pays to choose indigenous rock that's less expensive and doesn't have to be hauled across country. Boulders and slabs are priced by the ton, whether sold individually or by the pallet or truckload.

Special heavy equipment and hydraulic strength are necessary to lift and move most boulders. This is a job for a stone yard's delivery service—likely a boom truck with a crane or a sturdy backhoe that has the capacity to lift and place a boulder.

Native outcroppings hold forth on a site where the house was designed to nestle among the rocks. Colorful perennials are grouped to catch rain as it runs off the rocks.

Water laps the rocky rim of a swimming pool made to appear as natural as possible. This poolscape features 160 tons of handpicked boulders.

MOVING A BOULDER

Although you might be able to hoist a bushel basket-size boulder, it's better if you don't take the risk of injury. Instead, use a steel bar as a lever to roll rocks up to 300 or 400 pounds and then pivot them into place. Two or three people can use a wheelbarrow, hand truck, or dolly to budge a 100- to 300-pound stone. In any case, avoid lugging it on a slope.

A lichen-covered ledge brings an impression of age to this perennial garden. Shallow-rooted sedum and coreopsis tolerate dry conditions.

Two large stone slabs were built into this wall, creating a long-lasting bench. Moss and lichens have decorated the stones over time, giving the bench a timeworn appearance.

BUILD A TUMBLED-PAVER BENCH

Build a rustic garden bench using stone-look concrete pavers and following a few basic steps. First, choose broad, flat, rectangular pavers, such as the tumbled concrete version shown, or comparable ones that suit your garden. To calculate how many blocks you'll need, have a rough idea of how large you want the bench to be. Based on the size of the blocks, multiply the number in each course, or layer, by the number of courses.

Once you choose a location for the bench, excavate 4 to 6 inches deep and wider and longer than the base of the bench. Fill the excavation with a layer of crushed gravel topped with a layer of pea gravel. Lay the first course for the bench on this base. Stack the pavers for each course in a pattern different from those below it to help interlock the levels. Lay the top layer of pavers to overhang the support pavers. Use landscape block adhesive, available at home centers, to secure the bench-top pavers, tamping

Take a Seat on a Stone Bench

Every garden needs a spot where you can sit and enjoy the view. A stone bench proves inviting and weather resistant. Your bench could be a single mass of stone. For a more traditional freestanding bench, set a wide stone slab on narrower slab supports, concrete legs, or another comparably solid and sturdy base. Upright slab supports should be buried 12 to 18 inches deep, then backfilled with pea gravel and packed soil. Or form an adequate base using stacked flat stones or a pair of boulders with surfaces flat enough to accommodate a bench stone.

Alternatively, consider combining materials such as stone supports with a wooden bench or a concrete bench seat. If you prefer seating with a backrest, options include a stone bench built into a wall or a boulder chair (carved or quarried). If you do not find a suitable split stone slab for a bench, consider having a piece of stone cut or carved for the purpose. A concrete or cast-stone bench can be made to your specifications.

For an extended sit, a stone bench may not be as comfortable as a cushioned seat, but it will provide a strong physical and visual presence in the garden. Place a bench where the view is most appealing. Ideally, situate your bench where it will receive warm morning sun and cool afternoon shade. If your bench site does not already include a stone floor, plant groundcovers or spread gravel to provide dry, mud-free footing.

This small seaside patio called for rugged materials that withstand ocean winds and salt spray. Stone slabs provide a carefree floor, table, and seating. Salt-tolerant plants soften the mass of stone.

Ornament Your Garden with Stone

The delight of decorating your landscape with stone accents compares to icing a cake. This is the fun part: Finish your design by selecting art pieces that have personal meaning and then giving them a place of honor in the garden. Although your garden's ornaments reward you with the pleasure of their beauty and charm, those made of stone proffer additional benefits.

Some stone accents have a more utilitarian purpose, such as a stream or fountain's water music or its appeal to wildlife. You might have your heart set on a granite sundial, an abstract marble sculpture, or an antique limestone trough. Choose stone pieces that speak to your sensibilities and your garden's style. Like art inside your home, each piece should resonate with meaning, serve as a reminder of a wonderful trip, or express the character of the region where you live. No matter how simple or ornate your garden's stone embellishments, when they reflect your personality, you'll likely smile and feel good whenever you see them. Keep your stone art collection small. A small garden may accommodate only one choice piece of appropriate size and scale displayed effectively.

Blocks of quarried limestone stack artfully and shape an unusual garden wall with a hint of playfulness. The wall is tall enough to create some privacy, and its openings allow air to circulate among plants.

Stone exudes strength and permanence. It stands up to weather and time, and often becomes more appreciable as it develops a patina of age. The work of art that you choose to be part of your home landscape will likely become an ornament for others to enjoy over the years. Unlike most plants, stone accents keep their appeal in the landscape year-round.

Once you begin a search, you'll find a wealth of sources for stone ornaments, from garden boutiques to architectural salvage and antiques merchants, importers, and landscape art galleries or fairs. Work with a reputable dealer of antiquities and get a guarantee for your purchase. Buy direct from artists or shop overseas from your desk by perusing selections online. You'll find a range of stone objects as well as stone-look pieces made from concrete or resin.

A chunk of basalt, cut and carved to form a shallow basin, nestles among plants and provides a sheltered water hole for birds.

ADD ACCENTS TO PROJECTS

Many stone projects can incorporate stone accents. Contrast is key to making the accent stones stand out. A pattern of large fieldstones set into a dry-stacked wall of 1-inch bluestone adds artistic flair. Or place a single large piece of flagstone in a sharply contrasting color in the center of a patio for decorative effect. Gravel pathways edged with cobblestone or flat, round river rock set on edge are classic examples of stone accents.

Stone accents can be as simple as stacking three beautifully round stones like these. Stacks of stones, called cairns, are an intriguing way to highlight the characteristics of favorite rocks.

Boxwood and groundcover carpet the soil around this cast stone urn. Whether they are stocked with colorful plants or left empty, cast stone urns are excellent focal points.

Turn a stone with a surface depression into a planting bowl like this by filling the reservoir with potting mix and adding succulent plants. Place intriguing details, like this stone planted with hen-and-chicks, where visitors are sure to see them.

Find the Perfect Spot for Stone Accents

You may already have just the place in mind for a stone accent. That quiet corner of the backyard where the path curves could be the perfect spot for a special sculpture. A tall piece of statuary could be tucked among the shrubs in the side yard as a reward for taking that route to the back patio. How many times have you pictured a pair of shapely stone urns flanking your home's front entry and brimming with blossoms? Opportunities abound for ornamentation with stone in every landscape.

Of course, where you locate a stone accent depends on how you want to use it. The placement of an art piece may encourage you and your guests to pause and savor the view there. On a large property, a stone accent offers a landmark: Come this way back to the house. A stone lantern accents an especially pleasing plant combination while distracting your view from a more unsightly part of the landscape. A stone basin, birdbath, or fountain incites activity and excitement as wildlife stops by to drink and splash while you enjoy the show.

Use plants to complement your stone art and heighten its impact. A strictly ornamental garden nymph deserves to stand out against an evergreen backdrop. A mossy cast-stone turtle would vanish beneath densely shaded plantings but creates a focal point when standing on a gravel beach at the edge of a pond. On the other hand, some pieces work well peeking out from plantings and providing a surprise for visitors. A small tree or flowering shrub can be used to frame an art piece. A patch of a low-growing plant such as lamb's-ears or dwarf catmint may provide the ideal platform for grounding it.

Raise your stone accent closer to eye level by placing it on a plinth or pedestal. Any type of stone or concrete base will hold a piece on a level surface off the ground. Although stone pieces are often too heavy for thieves to take, large ornaments vanish in the night all too often. Insure valuable garden art and ensure its safekeeping by displaying it in a more out-of-the-way place. Anchoring devices are available.

Ferns, coleus, and other shade-loving plants surround this petite cast stone statue. Make a new stone statue look like it has been in the garden for ages by situating it among established plants.

Small pieces of flagstone are mortared together to create this bird bath. Situated among flowering annuals and perennials, its water surface reflects nearby blossoms.

Landscape Visit: Bedrock Beauty

The key to success when gardening on bedrock: Think big. Faced with frustrating growing conditions on a cramped site, these homeowners in Victoria, British Columbia, transformed their landscape using boulders. After a rocky start, the garden's beauty is now set in stone and measured by the ton.

Once a gently sloping market garden, the site changed drastically when developers took a slice out of the hill and hauled off every bit of topsoil. What remained was a layer of shale and clay on top of bedrock—impossible to cultivate, even with a pickax.

When the homeowners acquired the place, they turned to landscape designers and commenced a transformation.

Boulders and stones of all sizes were brought in and placed with heavy equipment to imitate natural stone outcroppings. The boulders, especially a 5-ton specimen in the front yard, draw attention, but they also stabilize the slope and create planting pockets. An 18-inch layer of topsoil provides space for plenty of plants to take root. Bluestone slabs shape a meandering path between planting beds and connect the front yard with the back.

Boulders and stones of all sizes, interplanted with creeping thyme, dwarf conifers, and helianthemum, among other perennials, march up to the front door of this home in British Columbia, Canada.

A Pennsylvania bluestone path, softened with creeping thyme, turns a narrow side yard into an inviting route between the front yard and backyard. In the background stones step up the sloping backyard framed by a cedar privacy fence.

Glossary

Aggregate. Gravel or crushed rock. Often refers to the binding ingredients mixed with portland cement for concrete.

Annuals. Plants that live for one growing season, then die. Annuals are replanted each spring. Some annuals sow their own seeds to regenerate each season. (See *Perennials*.)

Base. A prepared layer of gravel (and sometimes sand) to support paving material.

Batter. The inward slope from bottom to top on the face of a wall.

Batter gauge. A tapered board attached to a level to measure the batter of a wall.

Bluestone. A dark, blue-gray granite.

Bonding stone. A long stone that spans from one face to the other to tie a wall together. Also called a bondstone.

Boulder. A large stone, usually round or egg-shape, weathered, and worn smooth.

Bowl fountain. A water feature with one or more bowls, usually on a central stem. Water, which sometimes sprays into the air from the top, spills from one bowl to the next, and often pours into a pool beneath the fountain.

Calcite marble. A decorative stone of crystalline calcium carbonate that is embedded with colored silicates.

Capstone. The top course of stone on a wall or the flat top stone on a pillar or post.

Cobblestone. A medium-size, naturally rounded stone used for paving.

Cut stone. Quarried stone cut to uniform-size squares and rectangles for paving.

Diopside. A decorative green to white stone consisting of pyroxene.

Dry-laid. A stone patio or path laid without mortar, usually on a sand and gravel base.

Dry-stacked. A wall constructed of stacked stones without mortar.

Fieldstone. Smooth granite rocks, round or oblong, 6 to 24 inches in diameter, found on the ground or partially buried.

Fines. Powdery residue from mechanical crushing, found in crushed gravels.

Flagstone. Flat slabs of limestone, quartz, sandstone, or other kinds of stone. The slabs are often large but are easy to split. Flagstone is used for paths, patios, walls, and other projects.

Footing. A below-grade concrete slab or compacted gravel surface that supports a stone wall or other structure.

Fossilized rock. Decorative rock with fossilized remains of flora or fauna.

Frost heave. The upward movement of soil caused when moist soil freezes.

GFCI. Ground fault circuit interrupter, a device that instantly cuts off electricity when it senses an unbalanced flow in the hot and neutral wires, as in a short circuit. The pump of a water feature must be plugged into a GFCI for safety.

Grade. (noun) The level of the ground at a project site. (verb) To change, level, or smooth the surface of the ground.

Granite. Hard, natural, igneous rock that contains quartz and forms of crystalline feldspar.

Gravel. Small, loose rocks. Natural gravel often comes from rivers; rocks are smooth and rounded. The rocks in crushed gravel, made by mechanically crushing larger rocks, are more irregular and jagged.

Hisingerite. A decorative rock; black to brownish black with yellowish brown streaking.

Landing. An intermediate surface between stairs or staircases. Stairs often change direction at a landing.

Landscape fabric. A nonwoven fabric that allows water and air to pass through but blocks weed growth. Landscape fabric is a better choice than plastic sheeting for landscape construction.

Limestone. A versatile stone made mostly of calcium carbonate, formed mainly from shells and other organic remains.

Mortar. A mixture of one part sand, one part portland cement, and enough water to make a thick paste; used to set stone for patios, walls, and other projects and as grout between stones.

Mosaic. A surface of small stones of various colors and other materials, usually set in mortar.

Outcropping. A boulder placed in a landscape so it looks like a natural development.

Paver. Stone cut to uniform size for use in paths or patios.

Perennials. Plants that live more than one season. Perennials don't need to be replanted every year. (See *Annuals.*)

Plumb. The condition that exists when a surface is exactly vertical.

Pond liner. Rubber sheeting placed in a pond excavation to prevent water from draining through the soil. The flexible liner conforms to surface contours, so you can make ledges for plant containers inside the pond.

Primary pathway. A main travel route through the yard, such as from the driveway or public sidewalk to the front door of the house.

Quarried. Stone broken from a large, natural deposit, usually in an open excavation. Limestone, slate, and others are quarried.

Quartzite. Hard, light-colored, natural rock made of quartz and sandstone particles. Usually looks crystalline and sparkly on broken faces.

Rebar. Steel rod of various widths used to reinforce concrete and masonry.

Retaining wall. A wall constructed to prevent soil behind it from sliding down a slope.

Riprap. Rough, jagged pieces of quarried stone, which can be stacked to make rustic walls. Smaller than traprock, riprap is commonly used in civil engineering to stabilize slopes, stream banks, and similar projects. (See *Traprock.*)

River rock. Medium-size stones smoothed by river or lake water.

Rock garden. A landscape feature that combines stone and plants.

Rubble. Mixed rocks of various shapes and sizes used to fill between faces of a wall.

Ruin. A new stone feature constructed to look like one that has crumbled with age.

Sandstone. A sedimentary rock that usually contains quartz sand. Flagstones are often large pieces of sandstone.

Scree. A feature that resembles the piles of loose stones found in nature at the foot of the hill or the bottom of a cliff.

Screed. (noun) A straight board that is pulled over sand or concrete to level the surface. (verb) To level a surface with a screed.

Secondary pathway. A pathway that is not a main travel route through a landscape, such as a path through a flower garden.

Slab. A stone feature arranged to resemble a large, single stone outcropping that has split into fragments over time.

Slate. Dense stone formed in nature by compression of sedimentary rock; flagstones are often large pieces of slate.

Spill stone. The stone water flows over for a waterfall. Also called a lip rock.

Stepper. A piece of flagstone small enough to use as a stepping-stone. (See *Stepping-stone.*)

Stepping-stone. A flat stone large enough for a footstep, used to construct a path.

Stone step. Stone cut or split to size for use as a step or in a staircase.

Swale. A shallow depression in a landscape used to collect runoff.

Tamper. A tool used to compact soil or other base material.

Terra-cotta. Brownish orange fired clay used to make decorative plant containers and statuary.

Traprock. Large quarried rocks with jagged shapes and rough surfaces, used for wall construction. Commonly used in highway construction. (See *Riprap.*)

Tumbled stone. Rocks that have been smoothed by rotating a quantity of them in a revolving cylinder.

Underlayment. A nonwoven synthetic fabric placed under a rubber pond liner to prevent punctures and tears.

Wall stone. Quarried rock, usually limestone, cut into rough blocks for wall construction.

Special Thanks
Country Landscapes, Inc.
Ames, IA 50010
800/794-9795
countrylandscapes.com
See the fire pit designed and built by Country Landscapes, Inc., on page 101.

A combination path of flagstones and gravel meanders through this perennial garden. When selecting plants for your pathside gardens, refer to the chart at right for plant hardiness information.

USDA PLANT HARDINESS ZONE MAP

This climate zone map helps you select plants for your garden that will survive a typical winter in your region. The United States Department of Agriculture (USDA) developed the map, basing the zones on the lowest recorded temperatures across North America. Zone 1 is the coldest area and Zone 11 is the warmest.

Plants are classified by the coldest temperature and zone they can endure. For example, plants hardy to Zone 6 survive where winter temperatures drop to –10° F. Those hardy to Zone 8 die long before it's that cold. These plants may grow in colder regions but must be replaced each year. Plants rated for a range of hardiness zones can usually survive winter in the coldest region as well as tolerate the summer heat of the warmest one.

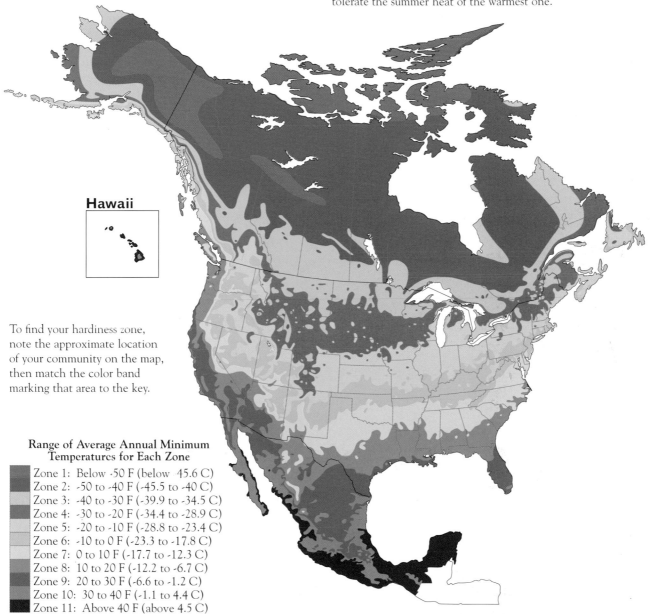

Hawaii

To find your hardiness zone, note the approximate location of your community on the map, then match the color band marking that area to the key.

Range of Average Annual Minimum Temperatures for Each Zone

Zone 1: Below -50 F (below -45.6 C)
Zone 2: -50 to -40 F (-45.5 to -40 C)
Zone 3: -40 to -30 F (-39.9 to -34.5 C)
Zone 4: -30 to -20 F (-34.4 to -28.9 C)
Zone 5: -20 to -10 F (-28.8 to -23.4 C)
Zone 6: -10 to 0 F (-23.3 to -17.8 C)
Zone 7: 0 to 10 F (-17.7 to -12.3 C)
Zone 8: 10 to 20 F (-12.2 to -6.7 C)
Zone 9: 20 to 30 F (-6.6 to -1.2 C)
Zone 10: 30 to 40 F (-1.1 to 4.4 C)
Zone 11: Above 40 F (above 4.5 C)

METRIC CONVERSIONS

U.S. UNITS TO METRIC EQUIVALENTS			METRIC UNITS TO U.S. EQUIVALENTS		
To Convert From	**Multiply By**	**To Get**	**To Convert From**	**Multiply By**	**To Get**
Inches	25.4	Millimeters	Millimeters	0.0394	Inches
Inches	2.54	Centimeters	Centimeters	0.3937	Inches
Feet	30.48	Centimeters	Centimeters	0.0328	Feet
Feet	0.3048	Meters	Meters	3.2808	Feet
Yards	0.9144	Meters	Meters	1.0936	Yards

To convert from degrees Fahrenheit (F) to degrees Celsius (C), first subtract 32, then multiply by $\frac{5}{9}$.

To convert from degrees Celsius to degrees Fahrenheit, multiply by $\frac{9}{5}$, then add 32.

Index

Welcome Home

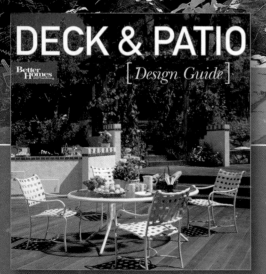

DECK & PATIO
[Design Guide]
Better Homes and Gardens

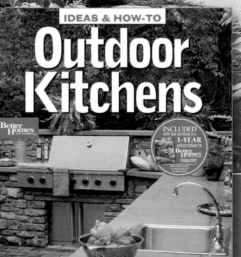

IDEAS & HOW-TO
Outdoor Kitchens
Better Homes and Gardens

INCLUDED with your purchase is a **1-YEAR** subscription to **Better Homes** magazine

Grills · Fireplaces · Lighting · Landscaping

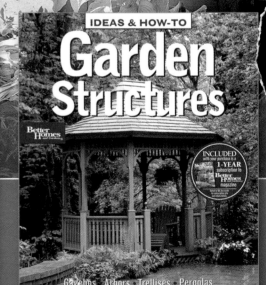

IDEAS & HOW-TO
Garden Structures
Better Homes and Gardens

INCLUDED with your purchase is a **1-YEAR** subscription to **Better Homes** magazine

Gazebos · Arbors · Trellises · Pergolas

Expert **advice** + **inspiration** + **ideas** + **how-to** for designing, building, maintaining your home's beautiful exterior